# Reflections in a Mirror

### D.V. Taneja

Copyright © 2014 D.V. Taneja
All rights reserved

Published by Purna Elements
www.purnaelements.org

ISBN: 978-0-9891286-2-9

*To you, Jawahar,
the treasured jewel among men,
I dedicate my book*

# Table of Contents

|  |  |  |
|---|---|---|
|  | Preface | ix |
| I. | Dedication | 1 |
| II. | Before thee, Goddess of Learning, I kneel | 5 |
| III. | Who is there to stop the songs of my heart? | 7 |
| IV. | Hush! Hush! doubts surround my mind | 9 |
| V. | Rama | 11 |
| VI. | Krishna | 15 |
| VII. | Lord Buddha | 18 |
| VIII. | Jesus Christ | 21 |
| IX. | Kalidasa | 25 |
| X. | Gandhi | 28 |
| XI. | Jawahar and Freedom | 40 |
| XII. | The Unknown Face | 46 |
| XIII. | Has anyone got the answers and does anyone fully know? | 49 |
| XIV. | I write today of the conception, what is truth? | 51 |
| XV. | This Frame of Flesh | 57 |
| XVI. | Music | 88 |
| XVII. | Children come from the dreamland of wonder | 90 |
| XXVIII. | To the Young Women of India | 93 |
| XIX. | Oh woman, you are one half dream and one half true | 95 |
| XX. | Youth | 98 |
| XXI. | Why is the present running away without a kiss? | 99 |

| | | |
|---:|:---|---:|
| XXII. | Day! you rise as is put round your neck, a garland of the golden rays of the sun | 101 |
| XXIII. | Holi | 104 |
| XXIV. | So bashful became my boyhood eight years past | 106 |
| XXV. | When I grew to be eighteen, you suddenly came in my life to coincide with the birth of my love | 108 |
| XXVI. | Dream | 113 |
| XXVII. | So you have come | 114 |
| XXVIII. | When you are away | 117 |
| XXIX. | My fair friend, the sight of you is a wonderful thing | 118 |
| XXX. | When I would cease to see the light of the day | 119 |
| XXXI. | When I look upon the lot of the people around me | 120 |
| XXXII. | When in review of the present times | 121 |
| XXXIII. | Drowned in the humdrum of busy life | 122 |
| XXXIV. | When on return from many a distant sojourn | 123 |
| XXXV. | As I move along the years of my advancing age | 124 |
| XXXVI. | The journey to Taj is like a pilgrimage | 125 |
| XXXVII. | It is memory that is everything | 127 |
| XXXVIII. | Flying in an Aeroplane | 129 |
| XXXIX. | Today, I write in memory of an old and sweet past | 130 |
| XL. | My Dearest Friend! | 133 |
| XLI. | Today, I am bearing a burden of great sorrow | 134 |
| XLII. | Death has struck another untimely blow | 136 |
| XLIII. | When I think of the slender thread that holds my heart | 137 |
| XLIV. | Sleep | 138 |
| XLV. | We met at the border line | 141 |

|        |                                                      |     |
|-------:|------------------------------------------------------|-----|
| XLVI.  | India 1958 Exhibition                                | 145 |
| XLVII. | My own Punjab                                        | 146 |
| XLVIII.| Ganga                                                | 150 |
| XLIX.  | My most beloved Motherland                           | 153 |
| L.     | The Republic Day                                     | 155 |
| LI.    | Young ascetic, why do you exasperate me into defeat? | 157 |
|        | Glossary                                             | 189 |

# Preface

I published in 1963, fifty years ago, "Reflections in a Mirror" my fifty-one poems in English, which I had then written until 1961. In the Blurb, it was stated that "in India, English is not a literary language; it is rather the language of administration, politics and commerce…". As I mentioned in the Preface then structured by me, I implied that these poems were reflections of pictures that my mind could not contain but required an outlet from the outpourings of my heart.

All poetry to be meaningful is an outpouring of the heart. Are there any borders which become the limitations of the heart? And English being a foreign language might get circumscribed by the complexity of its different idiom.

I started writing my poems in English when boundless ideas surrounded my heart which forced me to think in English and then express myself in English.

I have by now a total of up to 1000 pages of typed poems in manuscript form including 180 pages in "Reflections in a Mirror". How rich is the English language that provides me the medium to express myself in a form that is full of metaphor and rhythm, sound and flexibility which continuously produces and add new words. This is what enables me to think with so much ease in various demanding disciplines of subjects so different from each other like space and sciences but expression in English has now gone into the history of languages.

English is the communications channel of the world. Today, two strangers from different backgrounds coming up from any two parts of the globe can traverse with each other on any subject if they know the English language. English is now the only language to be qualified and known as the international medium of transmission.

English has a vocabulary of countless words that take shape out of nowhere. It can correctly describe the difference between the roar of the sea and the roar of the lion. It is a language that welcomes new words from other languages when it fails to produce the right nuance of expression from its own dictionary.

English is a mighty colossus to which all languages of the world both written and spoken, pay obeisance.

When does any foreign spoken word repeatedly uttered over years and decades, acquire the respectability to stand shoulder to shoulder with the words in writing and imprint, English has laid down the most demanding rules before it permits entry into its exclusive club, presided over by pandits of English. But 'nobob' is not yet ready to occupy that honoured place.

The journey of a new thought current jumps in my mind in the shape of a few lines and unless they are recorded forthwith, those lines in the original concept are lost forever. I do not know in what treasure house those starting lines are mysteriously born and when power releases them in a sudden outburst of what, I call, conceptual phrases of clarity and introduction of my poem.

I write poems which reflect conflicts and concerns and pains and privacies on the moral touchstone of life. If unresolved, these are outstanding issues which would keep me in a state of torture, tension and self-suffering. To write about the beauty of the world would limit itself in the totality of the subject but the dismay that I go through which I face and get involved in, can only be extinguished when I fully describe those travails.

To start writing a new poem whose origins are not known, is not only a physical process of transcribing the first few introductory lines in my long handwriting, but also to record the spark that lit the mind in print. The burden of the concept stays within me like a mathematical problem for which I have to attempt to find the correct solution. The answer to the puzzle keeps on germinating in my mind. Until the full text of the poem gets composed in the days that follow, the weight of the subject stays within me as a pregnancy. Even if the full text is written, I need the full text in its printed version to sink within me. I call this the rough first edition of the poem. I pursue the unfolding of the meaning in the days that follow in an effort to give it a flow, grace and content. Whether the composition is to end at 10, 100 or 500 lines is a decision that is taken when the total substance of the poem has been incorporated in its complete format.

I would like to answer the question what is the difference in writing an essay in poem and in prose?

The mind plays a part in both the exercises but the heart gives birth to a poem. The thought tantalizes the body and seeks a release from the overwhelming unease, composure and calm and that takes the shape of prose. Poetry is delivered from the passion of an artist. Poetry is the fountain from which sprout themes that are endless is their stream.

A pertinent question: Whether the artist who has in his or her concept a painting or a sculpture he or she creates to live in a world of his or her dreams? He or she must create and put a finishing touch to the theme of his or her interwoven dream.

Poetry is the finalization of a statement in the most abridged form, arranged in the minimum choice of such words that stay close to each other in smell and sound. Poetry is a statement which cannot be made in any other way –

*"Who is there to stop the
songs of my heart?"*

When does a poet decide that his verse has reached its end? Like any other passion pushed by the heart, one must be satisfied having fully consumed and tasted it in its totality and its content. One must decide and consult the same heart that gushed the ever new lines to seal the final kiss.

Poetry is a marriage between emotion and perfection in the design and grand order of words.

The strength and success of a poem lies in its capacity to survive the span of time.

My ideas have shrunk having given place to my advancing age.

Hope is a constant fight between eternity and opportunity.

DHARAM VIR TANEJA
( धर्म वीर तनेजा )

# Dedication

When I look at the flowers that smile in my land;
When I look at the fruits sweetening in my land;
When I look at the children growing in my land,
I wonder if my land is different from any other land.

When I see how minds are blossoming into flowers;
When I feel how country is vibrating with activity;
When I find how men are engaged in many adventures,
I wonder if my land is different from any other land.

When I can express my mind in the manner of my choice;
When art can develop in the manner it may choose;
When things can go on as they like to do,
I wonder if my land is different from any other land.

Is there any land similar to my land?
Where so many people speak so many languages;
Where so many views are held by so many men;
Where every man looks so different from every other man,
And yet that land is known as one's motherland.

Is there any land similar to my land?
Where religions of the world live as neighbours;
Where men of different ways and views all together live;
Where unity is to be found in diversity of thoughts and views,
And yet that land is called one nation's land.

I do not know whether my land is different from any other land;
I do not know whether men here are different from any other men;
I do not know whether the land or men are similar to those in any other land.

But is there any land?
Where one man is so important to the land;
Where one man is loved by so many men;
Where one man is trusted by so many men;
Where one man is heard by so many men;
Where one man is near to so many men;
Where one man is adored by countless millions;
That man is jewel of a man;
That land is the jewel of all lands.

Here is the man—
Who has not known in his life,
What is falsehood?
Who has not known what is deceit?
Who understands not what is betrayal?
Who is away from what is known as craft?
Who is conservative among moderns;
Who is young among old;
Who is present among past;
Who is future, present today.

As he lives amongst us;
As he is one of us;
We know not, how great he is?
How superior he is?
How higher he is?
How unmatched he is?

Those who know him say,
He is gentle like civility,
Fine like nobility,
Magnanimous like the universe,
And determined with a strong purpose.

There are many like him—
Who made their lands free;
Who brought strength and life to a weak nation;
Who made a nation throb with vibration.
But is there any one?
Who claimed for himself no special privilege and position;
Who gave up everything to serve his suffering brethren;
Who is just there because he has nothing else to do except to serve the nation.

If he is in power—
Those around him know not
What to do with him,
He is a jewel;
They have to treasure him.

How many there are in the world—
Whom their enemies love;
Who ever evoke admiration and respect;
Whose esteem mounts every day;
Whose regard improves with every step.
Who are just there;
And who remain there.
Thus my land is different from every other land.
My land has a jewel among men,
And the jewel makes the land different from every other land.

To you, Jawahar, the treasured jewel among men, I dedicate my book.
Prince among patriots,
Faultless and perfect artist,
Devotee of peace,
The best example of a man,
Strong, chivalrous and wise,
Unrivalled and unmatched in the annals of the world.

Having made an attempt to inscribe in verse what I could say;
Having poured my heart in a few little poems that I could create;
I wanted some light in whose brightness they could shine;
I wanted an example in whose perfection they could stand.
There is no brighter light that shines in the world than Nehru emanates.
There is no one more perfect to provide an inspiration than Nehru's name.
We, who live in his age, can feel the thrill of his existence.
We, who can see and hear him, can feel the ecstacy of his presence.
We are the blessed ones for we know the beauty of his life.
There is no greater inspiration for the artists of the world than Nehru's life.
My humble book is a poor dedication to that masterful mind.
May it partake a little of the glory that in his name shines.

## II

# Before Thee, Goddess of Learning, I Kneel

Before thee, Goddess of Learning, I kneel.
My country has its slavery given up,
And wakes up as the Sun of our freedom
Returns from its sojourn, where ill luck,
Devils of disunity and demons of lethargy held it back.

Now that there is light, the soul flutters at its sight,
And, in waking, makes a mighty effort to shed its weariness.
The conches are blown, the temples bell ring,
The populace in costumes bright and gay come out,
And make merriment to herald this long awaited day.

At your feet, Goddess of Learning,
Whenever this country was blessed by golden rays of freedom,
She drew from you her prayer, and what truly made her great.
I bow and beseech thee to grant us our prayer—
Let us be great.

Let us be great in wisdom to forgive—
In knowledge the other man's view to understand,
To our enemy love, to our life respect;
To produce more and to hold aloft
The banner of our peace-loving ways—
To be humble in profundity of our knowledge,

To be beside those who are weak and meek,
To be engaged in endless pursuit of truth,
To practise the highest forms of arts,
And to be truly great in music, poetry and stage.
India should become its own.
India should discover its soul.
India should be truly great.

# III

# Who is there to stop the songs of my heart?

Who is there to stop the songs of my heart?
Till the end of my life, from the prison of my heart,
Let them pour out their love, their anguish and smart.
Can any one ever stop the songs of my heart?

Why should my heart be ever grieved or ever lament?
Why should my mind be imprisoned ever at all?
Why should my soul be fastened to any one idea?
Why should any one put a stop to the songs of my heart?

Why should any fears ever visit my little mind?
Why must any doubts ever creep in my lonely heart?
Why should my soul ever flutter in being restless?
Am I not always in tune with the songs of my heart?

Over the vast lands of the world which I will visit;
Over the many wide seas which I will have to traverse;
Over the many hills and dales that I will have to cross,
I will continue to sing the songs of my heart.

My songs are born as I walk along.
From somewhere my unknown songs visit my heart.
My songs dance on my lips as I muse along.
How can I stop my songs when they sing in my heart?

I sing without effort and without any one's orders.
I sing for today and for the pleasure of the morrow.

I sing for my love and for those who love me.
I sing for nothing as nothing ever possesses me.

I will continue to sing till future is with me.
I will continue to be happy till life is in me.
I will continue to be restless till thinking is in me.
I will continue to be hopeful as love is in me.

Who is there to stop the songs of my heart?
I was born to sing the songs that rise in my heart;
I am living to sing the songs that dance in my heart;
I will die singing the songs released by my heart.

# IV
# Hush! Hush! doubts surround my mind

Hush! Hush! doubts surround my mind.
They say this is no poet's time.
This mechanised age knows no flirtings with men's thoughts.
People want more food, more wealth and more and plently.
Let men be free and possess equal rights.
Some say—Let men share in equal what men possess and make.
Others say—To each by his efforts what one can make.
But all around men want more of wealth.
This is a mechanized age and every one is in great haste.
No one has time to look back, no one has time to waste.
There is no stop or a pause for flirtings with men's thoughts.
Men can all produce, all the wealth and all the goods.
Such is the power of science and results of the mechanized age
That any one since Alladin's time could have through his magic lantern dreamt.
When men can all produce, let them; and what if they disagree;
They can fight with weapons, deadly weapons,
Guns, planes, and now atom bombs.
They may annihilate us all, never think of that;
Why should any one think at all?
When men can all produce, all the wealth and all the goods.
Men say—This is no poet's time.
The mechanized age knows no flirtings with men's thoughts.

Poet—Oh! this is the devil's mind that speaks.
There can also speak the poet's mind that is in you.
Let there be mechanized age, but why the man be its slave,
And why should one forget its maker—the man.
Why forget the man, the man who is born from one—
From one's mother who gives all her smiles and all her love;
One who has a large heart, and who lives, and lets live,
And who showers on her son all the love she can ever feel.
It is that love which, if it remains alive,
Determines the fact whether the poet in a man will rise.
Do not forget that one like mother, who can give,
Being full of it, as a mother is, of all deep love,
And gives all of it, he lives in bliss.
Man, you are a gift of love, gift that your mother gave,
And you will live in grief unless you pass on the gift.
Thus by a similar act pass on the gift.
A load lies on your breast, unless you part with it
How can you happy feel?
Pass on the gift of love that your mother gave.
Pass on that love to the woman you love,
To your daughter and son, to your neighbour, foe and friend,
To every one you can give, to any one you do know,
Give every one your love, and be blessed by it.

I wonder if a man could love, only love and love,
And his bride could plunder all the love he has in him,
And his children inherit nothing but just his love.
Then he will never have time to indulge in any war.
And then the poet in him will rise,
And this discovery will amaze—that a man is made of love.

We fight when springs of love go dry.
Let us fill them back and the poet in us will rise.

# V

# Rama

Deep inside in the recesses of human mind there are
many folds of qualities in all women and men,
And deeper still in the core of hidden folds there is a
diamond that shines in some rare and chosen men.
That diamond is the brilliant light that when it shines,
It puts to sorry shame the most brilliant sun-shine.
That diamond is the final thing that men aspire to unfold
By incessant penance, and in reaching the stage which is
the final goal.
When what they perceive with their inward light is not
seen by any human eye;
When they become possessed of what is noble and pure
any-where in human life;
When there is nothing higher that any man may ever
aspire to reach in his mortal life;
Then shines that diamond brilliantly and other men bow
to what they see
That God has appeared Himself to shine through his
chosen one so brilliantly.
Thus we, the men of *Bharata*, think of you, Rama,
As one diamond shining brilliantly.

Rama, you showed a man could also be God;
And thus, Rama, you threw a challenge to every man.
And every man, till today, thinks of you and looks inside,
And inside he examines his mind to see how he is far
behind?
And he cries in shame 'Rama I am far behind'.
And Rama, born in hoary distant past,
You still hold powerfully the minds of men in your grasp,

And they all think of you and say, "Rama, you alone could do.
"You alone could observe the code of *Dharma*,
"You alone could be the perfect man,
"You alone could be the example of what should be a man."
Every man tries to respond to that brilliance by being a different man;
Every one wants to be a better man to be near you, Rama,
And to be blessed by a part of your brilliance, and to be your chosen one, Rama.

Rama, the diamond shining brilliantly is a call to every man;
A call from shining brilliance to the brilliance hidden in every man.
But Rama, covered by the folds of limitations of human frame,
Men cannot see the brilliance of your shining diamond.
Trying hard, as they do, to come near you they remain the faulty humans,
Because all over they feel the limitations that make them remain as humans,
The limitations that, Rama, you alone could discard;
The limitations that we human fallen, falling, fallible fail to discard.
And thus, Rama, you remain the idol, the ideal of every mind,
And every one, Rama, remembers you and thinks of you.
And every one thinks that you would once visit his mind,
And let him have a glance of your shining brilliance.
To be blessed by that brilliance and to wear a part of your glow,
To learn from the example of your sacrifice, and to be inspired by your perfect role.

Rama, you shunned cosy comforts of a palace, and you gave up the right to rule.
You stood for what was right, and you stuck to what was true.
All you did, all you ever said, no man could ever do.
And thus Rama, born as a man, you lived as God and men still bow before you.
Rama, from distant past, you stand as the great moral giant;
And we dwarfs walk meekly and slowly in the shadow of your super strength.

Rama, you let those, who were nearer you, acquire a part of your glow.
You released such energies that those, nearer you, were made doubly pure.
And thus were born the immortal names of Sita, Lakshmana, Bharta and Hanuman.
All these stand for us as symbols of their specialities,
And we men think of you and think of them wondering at their qualities.
And we men think of the immortal epic telling your noble tale,
And we feel the strength of your brilliance by singing the songs of your tale;
Inspiring us, calling us to march behind your glorious trail,
To be blessed by the sound of your holy name,
And by the knowledge of your ever lasting fame.

And in this way, Rama, our land, our people, our women and men are blessed by you.
Ever inspired by the strong brilliance of your matchless observance of *Dharma*,
And shining through the strong and pure form of your

diamond *Karma*,
You, Rama, are the moving spirit behind the teeming millions of *Bharata*,
Who look up to you in dedication of the great example set by you.
And thus, if *Dharma* has never been extinct from our noble *Bharata*,
It is because, Rama, *Dharma* incarnate, you shine like a diamond brilliantly.

# VI

# Krishna

In India's endless span of time,
In India's old and mystic past,
No one has cast a greater spell;
No one has been a greater power;
No one has been a greater man;
No one has been a source of greater strength—
His name, his romance, his deeds and his thoughts
Are known all over the land.
He is no one but India's cherished name,
Spoken, spelled, chanted, and known Krishna,
The God amongst men.

Every man, woman and every one has a picture of this
enchanting man.
He is the strength of every soul,
And he is the symbol of perfection for every man.
Such is the unusual magic spell in which he holds every
one in this land.

From the date of his birth till the time of his death he was
destined to deal with evil minds.
He knew how barbaric could be a cruel man and how
simple and noble a pure mind.
Thus, no one in the world has ever keenly felt the misery
of any human mind,
Thus, no one in the world has been ever known who
reached the depth of every human mind,
Thus, all over the land, men and women knew here was a
man whom they could trust,
Here was a man who knew earlier than them the agony

and conflict they ultimately faced;
Here was a man who placed before every one the right path that lay ahead of him.
Such vast was his knowledge, such sagacious was his wisdom,
Such overwhelming and powerful was his command over human mind,
And such compassion and love overflowed in his boundless heart that it flooded the entire universe.
Thus, any one he spoke to, any one he looked at, and any one he thought of
Was blessed, and freed of his confusion and grief of his mind.

He gave the world the gift of his essence.
He made the world understand the life's intent.
He made the world a place worthy to live and spend.
He made every one a holy man, and thus gave him strength
To withstand what was unholy in him.
He made the man an instrument of supreme design.
He gave the man the dignity he knew not how to find.
He said "Obeisance to *Dharma* is the prime purpose of life.
"Surrender not your conscience to the immediate gains of life.
"There is a truth that prevails supreme over all conflicts of life,
"And the present phase of living is but a brief halt in the endless chain of life."
His message was eternal and immortal.
"Choose the path that righteousness dictates.
"Compromise not with evil, and follow the path clear and straight."
In every one's life a crisis comes when one knows not

what to do.
But Krishna gave a clear answer,
"Believe in the eternity of the universe, whatever else you may do."

Krishna carved a place in the heart of every man;
Such was the unusual spell of this mystic on the minds of men.
He was as great as any God, and he was as great as any man.
His spell lies in his dual self, He is greater than any God or any man.
Whether he has ever had a garb of human frame,
And whether he ever walked the wide expanse,
Is not what has ever concerned any one.
Every one believes he ever lives,
And he is more alive than any living man.
He is stronger than any one the world has ever known
Because he is in the heart of every man.

# VII

# Lord Buddha

When the country had become mad by an over-dose of ritualism;
When prejudice, hate and bigotry were practised as religion;
When people vied with one another in exhibiting hollowness of their wisdom;
When men were seized by a craze for showing acute formalism;
When animals were sacrificed to propitiate gods of happiness;
When blood was used as a symbol of valour and bravery;
When men were cruel and violent even with their fellow men;
When peace was practised by waging many barbaric and meaningless wars;
When knowledge was made perverse to propagate ignorance and stupidity;
When men had lost altogether their vision of simple truths and commonsense;
When hearts throbbed to pick up quarrels for display of one's vanity;
And when the nation was divided into many camps of chaos and confusion;
Buddha, you were born to cry a halt to this march towards disaster.
Buddha, to let the country rediscover its soul you took your birth.

Buddha, in those times
When minds of men were heavy with thoughts of bitter

enmities and conflicts;
And when killing was considered sacred and the minds of men were perverse,
It would have been well nigh impossible to turn the minds of men from their evil pursuits.
But you sensed the doubts of men, you knew it would not be an easy task to melt the hardened hearts,
And therefore, Buddha, you turned your eyes inside to discover the truth;
You burnt to purify yourself to realize the truth.
In that penance you found that reason had fled from the minds of men;
That humility, forgiveness and sanctity were not practised as virtues divine;
That humans had just ceased to be humane,
That men could not love other men, being full of hate and prejudice;
That barriers of caste were raised to divide man from man,
And those born in low castes were considered as sub-human.
Then your mind was torn with grief and your heart overflowed with sympathy.
Then you saw how simple truths had got entangled in the web of intricate verbiage,
And when you separated them, they stood out as pure and shining gems,
And then the world learnt that Buddha, who had attained enlightenment, had been born,
And the path that the people had lost, and Buddha then showed, was the right one.
Not one of high-sounding philosophies and incomprehensible scriptures,
But of simple truths of love, purity, forgiveness, tolerance and simplicity.

And therefore, Buddha, when the nation discovered its soul, it stood in silent humiliation of its sins.
Not only did our own land learn the truths but wherever tyranny seized the minds of men,
The voice of Buddha traveled faster then the demons of tyranny,
Making Buddha the immortal and privileged son of the wide universe.


Buddha, who can ever measure the extent of your greatness?
Who can ever visualize the strength of your glory?
Is there any one, in whose life-time, compassion had echoed in the heart of every one?
Is there any one, after whose death, masses were moved to such intense dedication?
Even today when the world is rent with conflicts;
Even today when the world needs a balm to soothe the pain of its wounds,
The soul of Buddha blesses it with its boundless compassion,
Making the world a place worthy to live in.

# VIII

# Jesus Christ

For millions in the world it is time to recall the day
When you, Jesus, were born in the hush of tyranny.
When the poison of malice and bitterness was
overflowing to the brim;
When men, women and children were trampled and
crushed to death
For their love for righteousness, and for just the freedom
to hear the truth.
When those, who practised naked barbarism, were
considered as civilised men;
When brutal violence was upheld as the last word in any
argument.
In those times, you were born, a tiny little thing, to face
the mighty strength of a great power.
And every year, today, the world sits up and prays—
Jesus! Glory be to you,
You, the son of the Lord, chose this day to bless the
world.

There, in the dark deserts of Bethlehem, a light was lit
Which butchery, tyranny and violence could not put off.
And in those arid surroundings a God was born
Who showed the world a path to be followed by it.

Jesus, you made man an individual he was not before.
You laid the foundations on which the present edifice of
great civilization is built—
The love for truth, the spirit for sacrifice, the prize of
individual liberty and the freedom to think;
For all these qualities, Jesus, you died so that the world

could live.
Jesus, you showed to the world that it is worthwhile to die;
Whenever dignity, respect and values of life are threatened;
Whenever men are blinded by passion for absolute power;
Whenever reason is divorced and veil of ignorance shrouds the minds of men;
Whenever a false sense of prestige drives them to commit heinous crimes;
Whenever they persecute the world to chisel it in one form and shape;
Whenever those who show the path of forgiveness, love and compassion are considered as enemies;
Whenever evil is preferred to good, and falsehood to truth;
Whenever those who conspire and hold aloft ignoble means, are worshipped as gods;
And when mercy is looked upon with derision, and patriotism treated with jeers.
Such was the challenge, Jesus, that you faced in your life,
And you took up the challenge and you chose to die
Than to submit to bondage of body and spirit;
Than to live as a coward in defeat of your ideas;
Than to bow before torture, curse and fear;
Than to discriminate between a man and a man
For colour and form, creed and class;
Than to praise the rich as wise, and condemn the poor as ignorant;
Than to give Caesar what was not his, and not due to him.
Jesus! you thought that it was better to die in heroic glory
Than to live in insult and humiliation.

For all this, Jesus, you lived up to what you ever said
So that those who had faith in you did not feel
That a man greater than you could ever be born;
That there would be one known, till the sun would be there to give its light and warmth;
Till the moon and stars could be seen by human-beings;
Till then Jesus, the world would know that you were the only one
Who stood up and said, "I fear not any one except my own conscience."
For Jesus, the greatest in you was your courage and fearlessness,
For the mightiest in the world knew not what more they could do
Than to kill you.
And after your death those who conspired to kill you
Found you greater than when you were not dead.
Oh, they regretfully cried to have rather seen you live than die,
For they stained their hands red with your innocent murder,
The indelible stains that are seen till today on the cross that you bore,
The cross that has ever led the masses of men on the path of deliverance,
The cross that has been upheld as the symbol of your proud and dignified defiance.
Jesus, your death was like the mighty tide of a stormy sea
That engulfed in its sweep all your pigmy enemies,
Washing them clean of the sins that they bore in their enmity,
And blessing them by an absolute pardon of their utter stupidity.
But, Jesus, is it not true? that

All the noise of living and all the mighty efforts for existence
Appear pale offerings to the cause of being born,
For birth is indeed the greatest event in the life of any one,
And death is the only natural end to everything that is born.
Thus, Jesus, your birth was beyond doubt a great event,
And in gratefulness we remember it.
But you, Jesus, made living so noiseless and death such a mighty event
That it was only right that you should have been crucified.

But today, the day, when you were born the world rejoices,
For what could have been a greater event till today
Than the grace that you were born and we live today?

# IX

# Kalidasa

Kalidasa, were you ever really born?
King of dreams, not one airy tale of your fantasies could ever be told by any human mind.
So, how can I believe that you were really ever born?

No one was ever born who had such a beautiful face,
Such heart that was so endless in its yearnings and so unfathomable in its love,
As of Shakuntla, the heroine of your epic poem.
Thus, Kalidasa, the pictures you painted cannot be held on any canvas.
How can then I believe that you were really ever born?

Kalidasa, you did not even say one thing that I could believe.
How could clouds carry hearts as those of men?
How could they weave songs that only you knew?
And how did they send messages that only you understood?
You often said things that were incomprehensible to my mind.
Thus how can I believe that you were really ever born?

Kalidasa, they even dispute the place where you were born,
And even the time when you were born.
How can then you claim to be among the world's best men?
I am afraid I cannot believe that you were really ever born.

Kalidasa, even believing that you were ever born
You must have been a different man.
You must have woven such doping songs as to make
others lose their sense of tide and time.
And you must have cast a magic spell that men believed
in what you ever said,
And therefore no one did ever question that you were
really ever born.

Kalidasa! your poems are like the realm of the unknown;
Where shadows also talk, where love becomes misery,
and pleasure, suffering;
And under an unbelievable spell the men are made to
believe in what they are told;
And as if before a master-hypnotist they are made to
believe as also made to do.
Like that, Kalidasa, you hold the men in sway of your
super strength.
Pray, release that bond, unfetter the minds of men from
your magic spell.
We are held in continuous suspense about the fate of
your participants—
Who have bound us so tenderly with them that neither
force nor requests are of any avail,
Unless, Kalidasa, you break the spell of that tender bond,
That soft and silken love that we have for your brave and
beautiful cast.

Kalidasa! you were the master-poet, the greatest dreamer
who was ever born,
And your fantasies are like the realities of one's treasured
dreams.
Having been uplifted to the fairy-land of your
Rhapsodies

We are face to face with those who fill the air with their sweet ecstasy,
And who invite from our hearts sympathy and love too tender for words.
And in that air of suspense, Kalidasa, you hold us in a state of utter helplessness,
Weak, unable to speak even a single word;
Overwhelmed by the exquisite beauty of your masterly creations.
We, mortal men witness a sight that we are unable to describe,
And that is the greatest achievement of your artistic creations.

Kalidasa, you have been the greatest poet of our motherland.
No matter whether you were really ever born, no matter whether you lived at all,
You are still the greatest and the most beloved poet of our motherland.

# X

## Gandhi

In India's ageless, dateless life she once did discover her soul.
In India's known and unknown past she once did discover herself.
Once in her life lived a rare man who mirrored all her hoary past;
Once in her destiny came a wonderful man who called a halt to her hazy path;
Once in her history arrived a perfect man who made history a jewelled past;
Who was so great that he was just unconcerned of his being great,
And that made greatness a little unknown thing.
Who reduced thinking to such an effortless thing
That intellectuals knew not how to keep pace with his thinking.
Who was so humble
That humility often felt ashamed to face him.
And as long as he lived he made the nation pulsate and vibrate with his living.

For over two thousand years the country had been often split.
Often she had bled, and often her soul had been put to cruel tests.
Often aliens had foisted their foreign faiths, and often had they changed the country's face.
Often the nation had tried to change its fate but often failed.
For centuries did the country make efforts to recover its

soul and choose the right path.
There was now and then a pause, but often we were deflected from our path.

When the nation was steeped in ignorance, minds wrapped in slavery;
When living was divided in camps and castes, and thinking made confusing by contradictions;
When courage was camp-follower of tall talk, and compassion of perverse cruelty;
When the poor were accused of being poor, and the rich lauded for being rich;
When the country was doped to sleep, and its mind made dead by lethargy;
When the country stood still, slowly gasping for breath, Gandhi, you arrived on the scene quietly and silently.

What was that that Gandhi did that others could not?
What was that that Gandhi saw and others had not?
What was that that Gandhi felt that others did not?
Gandhi did, saw and felt everything that others had not.

Gandhi attuned himself to the soul of true India.
Gandhi was moved by the agony and distress of mother India.
Before Gandhi rose India's past challenging him to choose his path;
Challenging him to propagate those views that would wake the nation's conscience;
Calling him to discover the truth that would show what India was?
Gandhi took up the challenge and undertook to stir the nation's conscience.
In the dumb millions of India's suffering villagers he found an image of God.

And in keeping before himself that God, he identified himself with their lot.
And in preference to any other cause he had their cause dear to his heart.
In a world torn by strifes and itching for another war
He preached *Ahimsa* in thoughts, words and deeds.
In a world full of selfish and tyrannical men he preached philosophy of love and truth.
In a world of fear, suspicion and doubt he preached trust and fearlessness
He was so brave that heroic deeds adorning history appeared pale.
He was so powerful that those who opposed him always felt a challenge.
So long as he lived, he tried to make his living an unknown phenomenon,
But for the world his living became the most important event.

Here was a special and wonderful man who spoke with a strong conviction;
Who spoke what he meant, and who did what he believed in.
Who only chose such words for his expressions that they only conveyed one meaning.
In this world of craft and double talk his artless talk was in strange contrast.
The simple words and casual remarks could cause the shake-up of big empires.
His enemies put such meanings to his words that he had never intended to convey.
His friends felt amazed that he used such simple words that nothing more they could ever explain.
But he stood laughing and joking despite what the people anywhere talked,

And he remained unconcerned of the interpretations they would put to his ideas.

Everyone felt here was a man who stirred his sleeping conscience.
Whether Gandhi was silent or spoke any words he always gave a challenge.
Whether one ever followed him or ever opposed him one had to stake everything;
While he was the same to his followers and enemies loving everything,
Yet no one knew what he would do as the next thing.
But every one knew, and he always proved that with a conviction he did everything.

Gandhi was a unique man the like of him may never walk this earth again.
He was the most perfect example of an individual.
All the world over there has not been one man of his parallel.
He started his life with himself.
He believed in building his own individual self.
He fortified himself by consolidating his own strength.
He believed that a powerful self was the best shield against one's own sins.
He was convinced that correcting oneself was a great achievement.
He knew masses only listened to one who practised what he preached.
In Gandhi it was difficult to find
Where what he practised merged with what he preached.

Gandhi was truthful to the core;
He was honest to the extreme;
He was simple to the infinity;

He was straight to the end.

There was no sphere of life that Gandhi did not touch.
Here was a man whose was a wholly successful life,
And holy he was, and holy he made everything wherever he went.

Gandhi led such a life that he became the noblest example to other women and men.
He ever looked peaceful and serene; he always wore a confident look;
And he became the best specimen of man that the world had ever produced.

Gandhi was a fearless man who knew not what danger was.
His bravery was that of an unarmed man who was prepared to die for a cause.
Who preferred death to a life of humiliation and insults,
And yet he considered living a sacred and solemn trust.

Gandhi could muster millions of men to follow him,
Yet he was not out for a following.
He presided over the hearts of millions of men,
But he tried not to influence even a single man.
He was selflessly selfless because he knew not anything else.
He thought every one important because he knew not what was unimportant.
He was so frank that no one knew how to talk to him in any way different.

He was as pure as Sita.
He believed in the code of *Dharma* of Rama.
He believed in the philosophy of *Karmayoga* of Krishna.

He believed in the principles of *Ahimsa* enunciated by Buddha.
He believed in the boundless compassion of beloved Jesus.
He believed in the burning faith of the Great Mohammad.
He believed in truth as the final form of *Parmatma*,
And he thought of life as a greatly precious thing to be a concern of everyone.

Here was a rare, perfect man who was greater than greatness;
Simpler than simplicity, purer than purity;
Of whom it was difficult to believe that he lived till he died;
And about whom no one would ever believe that he ever lived or died.
Gandhi merged living with death and death with living.
He was one such rare soul that he made living as noiseless as the act of dying.

Though in the beginning, it was asked, what was Gandhi before Great Britain?
But at last, the question became, what was Great Britain before Gandhi?
Gandhi appeared often single commander of a single man army;
And yet that single Gandhi was often stronger than the mighty arms of Great Britain.
Never has the world witnessed such an unequal fight,
But always without exception, and surely, it was Gandhi who won the fight.
Never in the history of the world were arms so useless;
Diplomacy so naïve, and subtlety without any benefit
As before Gandhi's truthful and straight methods and

non-violent strength.
Gandhi made politics religion; and made others fight him on his plane.
Others knew not how to fight him because they knew not the secret of his strength.

Gandhi was often put in jails,
But he made jailing a journey divine.
Never were jails so worthy a place;
Never were imprisonments so much of a pilgrimage.
Gandhi had said, "All journeys for the sake of one's conscience, "All sufferings undergone for one's beliefs "Were more purifying than journeys to see stones and shrines of one's pilgrimage."

The British knew not what to do with him, how to face him.
They had dealt all the world over with normal looking men.
Here was a man who tried to be straight and simple,
And appeared to them to be the most abnormal man.
They knew not whether by ignoring him he would be less great or by dealing with him.
They were always arguing whether they should first talk to him or he should start the talks.
Gandhi remained what he was;
To him it mattered not who initiated the talks.
He could converse as much in silence as in expression.
He had only one cause dear to his heart that of freedom for his beloved India.
He stood not on ceremonies, he wanted the British to quit India.
And he told them candidly so, when he thought the time had come for them to depart.

Gandhi did what he believed in;
He never did anything he did not believe in.
He fought what he opposed;
So he opposed all that was unjust in our or any one's ways.

He made living such a simple thing that one knew not why it was complicated.
He reduced desires to such a nothingness that one knew not what one needed at all.
He made thinking such an honest phenomenon that one knew not why men were cunning in thinking.

Those were the times of his active life when the very conscience of world was being questioned;
The times when science had put men's ideas and thinking into a new shape;
When the world had lost faith in the ultimate reality of an individual's personality;
When state had become all powerful, and man a small part of a giant machine.
At that time Gandhi raised his voice of protest.
He accepted the challenge thrown by state and science to the life of man.
He offered and put himself as one individual.
State could make no inroads in his life for he challenged it at every stage.
Science could not explain the reason of his survival when he lived without food for several days.
Gandhi showed that there was an innate power that determined finally the fate of the world,
And we were only His poor instruments who obeyed the power that really ruled.
For him state was a structure of lies, and science plaything of a curious mind.

He warned that since man was the strength behind his own creations,
He should not be allowed to be crushed by their weight.
He thought of every one as an individual state.
He said, "Surrender not your conscience.
"The state cannot call to question the minds of men.
"One must pursue pure, straight and clear ways."

Gandhi made every one noble and drew the best from him.
Models of clay became men of vision and of singular courage.
Gandhi could kindle in the land a new line of action.
He could infuse in the heart of every one a new line of thinking,
And he could stop the nation from following bad and ignoble ways.

Gandhi had faith in women because they were nearer his concept of a being
He waited for the day when they would really hold the reins of living.
He felt they were nearer the role that he expected an individual to play
In a nameless, shapeless and budgetless state.
He really wanted women to occupy their genuine honoured place,
The place of being rulers through their sweet, gentle and cultured ways.

Gandhi was really a zero man.
He was one who enhanced the value of being nothing.
He believed in a philosophy which was artless, true and pure like zero.
He injected in the life of every one a new hope, a new

vision, and a new courage
But he wanted himself to be forgotten by every one.
Once in thousands of years he made the country one and free from bondage.
But at that time he was far away, talking to suffering women and men.

Gandhi wanted not the power to stick to any one.
He believed in the collective wisdom of a large number of men.
He believed that sleeping conscience of men must be awakened.
He wanted to leave a heritage to enrich the goodness of men.

We live in his shadow and know not how great he was.
We are too small to know how big Gandhi was.
We are yet too near him to assess what his contribution was.
We know not how lonely the world feels without his ideas.
We grope about trying to assess what Gandhi was.

Gandhi showed before our eyes that immortality was in the hands of every one;
That victory was near at hand;
That the world was a worthy place;
That to save it must be the crusade's end.

Gandhi, you were a mater-man, a master-mind, and a master-soul
Who held in his armless sway the entire land.
At whose command the entire land throbbed as if in unison,
As if in common upsurge, in common feeling and in a common bond.

Gandhi, you wore no sceptre or crown;
You commanded no arms;
And yet, you moved kingdoms.
Empire of yesterday became Commonwealth of today,
And that alone could be a fair consummation of what you had ever preached.

Gandhi, as long as you lived you wanted the land to be one and free.
When you died it was to preserve the land to be one and free.
Had you done your task, had you achieved your destiny?
Had you fulfilled your mission, had you reached your goal?

You wore a mortal frame, and that was your only liability.
One day you had to depart, but you who challenged death at every step;
You, who proclaimed that living was in your hand,
Could only have died at an assassin's hand.
No other end could have better explained your viewpoint;
No other death could have better proved your strength.
All throughout you had said, "All men are one.
All belong to the same religion, the religion of brotherhood of man."
And when you died, it was in the cause of your protecting that brotherhood of man.

For us, Gandhi, your living was no doubt a mighty event.
We who lived in your times were the blessed ones,
For we witnessed and felt the power of a mind over fellow-ones.

But your death was greater then your living,
For when you died, death itself was crucified.
Every day that passes is a challenge to every one:
How great was Gandhi, and how he transcended the bonds of human frame.
And how we men, small in vision, dwarfed in intellect, and blunt in perception,
How we can fathom the ocean of his super strength?

Gandhi, the challenge is growing in measure everyday.
Everyday we walk away from the standards set by you;
Everyday we are making our task doubly hard,
And everyday we accept defeat and walk apart.
That time is not very far when we shall change our path
And tread the path so wisely shown by you.
Then for thousands of years you will be a guiding star,
And we, the men of your times, will be known as the blessed men.

# XI
# Jawahar and Freedom

As I move from place to place;
As I go from street to street;
As I see people from house to house;
I ask them all a question,
"Are you free?"
When I go out for a walk,
I speak to plants, flowers and trees,
I ask all of them the same question,
"Are you free?"

Often in my sojourns I come across many an animal,
Many birds and insects of every type,
Though they speak not my language, I am tempted to ask,
"Are you free?"

What is that type of freedom about which I ask?
About freedom to starve and about freedom to die;
About freedom to suffer and about freedom to weep;
About freedom to wake and about freedom to sleep.
No, I ask not about these freedoms.
Such freedoms are to us not denied.
I fear not about the loss of these freedoms.
But I fear about the loss of my personal freedoms.
The freedom to laugh and the freedom to smile;
The freedom to grow and the freedom to decide;
The freedom to concede and the freedom to deny;
The freedom to be wrong and the freedom to be right;
The freedom to believe in truth and the freedom to believe in lies.
It is for these freedoms that I ask each and every one this

question.

And each and every one tells me "I am fully free."
The flowers, plants and trees, birds, insects and animals,
Men, women and children,
They all tell me,
"We are fully free."

Who has given the country this freedom?
Who has ensured the land its security?
Who has created the atmosphere of breathing fresh air?
Who has made India one, free indivisible land?

Freedom was born in the heart of Jawahar when he was born.
And true to his heart, that has been his love all his life.
All his life he dreamt and breathed and fought for freedom,
And having brought freedom to our land, he wears the crown of its prize.

In this world convulsing with utter confusion,
Jawahar is trying to steer clear this ship of our State.
In this world split by acrimony of several arguments,
Jawahar is trying to keep a balance in the thinking of men.
In this world threatened by uncertainty writ large,
Jawahar has given India with certainty the blessings of her freedom.
In this world sitting on the brink of its own insecurity,
Jawahar has made India just one, vast haven of security.
Our land is full of many troubles creating confusion worse confounded,
But Jawahar is the master-performer preserving freedom in confusion,

Thus Jawhar watches this land grow mature in freedom,
Making freedom of this land an envy of this world.

Since over a decade when government in every country
has been once swept off its feet;
When in many a land the rulers know not the mind of
their masses;
When those inhabiting their lands know not when they
may meet their annihilation;
When no other nation knows what may befall next
second;
Jawahar, you have let India sit up and freely breathe.
You have given the nation its stature and self-confidence.
You have given the country its prestige and position.

People in India have moved about as if the world is in
perpetual peace.
People here do not fear about the hovering planes
Carrying death through atom bombs.
There is something, Jawahar, you have done that
provokes them not, those who hate.

Jawahar, what are you?
Who are you?
What is that that makes you a different man?
Bearing a catholic and cosmopolitan outlook,
Possessing a rare sagacity and deep wisdom,
Sympathetic to all and considerate to every one,
You know how men can get divided in many an
argument,
You know what causes so much distress and hate.
Your insight into the minds of men;
Your height in intellectualism;
Your being heads and shoulders above the other little
men;

All that lends your personality a unique, magical charm.

Often when you are silent; people are intrigued by what this silence means.
Is that an expression of disapproval and reproach?
People value your opinions, the scales can only be balanced by your fair assessment.
Thus everywhere, whatever the men may say, whatever they may do,
A question is asked again and again,
What about Nehru's views?
In the world you stand today as symbol of hope, as angel of peace;
Deliverer and saviour of mankind.
One, on whose counsel and views even conflicting nations are prepared to place faith.

Nehru, you derive your strength from what you have done for the nation.
Our India, made great by you, has made you greater;
Greater than any one the nation has ever placed before the world as its son.
Thus Nehru and India are two indivisible things,
Making India the great Nehru's beloved motherland.
Nehru is shaping India attuned to his soul.
A tolerant, wise, free, healthy and strong India is in Nehru's dreams.
What Nehru feels, thinks and dreams about India, he pours back into India.
All his ambitions, plans, schemes and dreams are around and about India.
Nehru has no personal, private and individual living;
He is only a part of the strong current of India's stream.

Nehru has made India the land of tranquility and peace,

free from fright and fear,
And given people freedom in abundance to feel and breathe.
He has let them enjoy the bliss of their own spiritual strength.
He has given everyone freedom to shape his individual living.
He has let everyone draw inspiration for his own existence.
He has placed no bars or handicaps in any one's pursuits.
He has not caused any one any injury.

The many religions sprout and grow in this land.
The artists live in abandon and enjoy the reverie of their own conceptions.
The travellers and tourists see the good and bad of this land,
And Nehru has let this land grow in the grandeur of its heritage.

Has the world ever produced a greater artist than Nehru is?
An artist dedicated so much to a cause; the cause of bringing freedom and joy to his fellow men.
Is his life not the best blend of the best qualities of men?
He is the one in complete harmony with the world around him;
He is the one whose words carry the pictures of the best imagery;
He is the one in whose voice rings the sweetest of melodies;
He is the one who has had the noblest of dreams ever dreamt;
He is the one who has brought solace to the hearts of the suffering-ones.

Who can match his breadth of vision?
Who can measure the depth of his sincerity?
Who can come near the largeness of his tolerance?
Who can compete the warmth of his love?
He is one such rare man in history;
Who has been admired and loved by his enemies;
In whose words his enemies have full faith;
In whose presence his enemies feel overwhelmed;
In whose integrity no one has ever cast a doubt.
Even when his enemies hate him in the vilest way,
They talk jealously of his qualities,
And when Jawahar faces them,
They know not how they had counted him as an enemy.

He is today the staunchest supporter of the British Commonwealth,
The Doyen of the family, pillar of its strength.
Yet often he had languished in British prisons
For inciting rebellion against the Britrish Crown.
There is no bitterness in his thoughts;
There is no rancour in his views;
There is no faltering in his decisions.
His resolves are strong, his views are balanced, his thinking is clear.

He never minces his words.
He never compromises with falsehood.
His friends know his weaknesses; his enemies know his strength.

Thus, Nehru, beloved of India, darling of the world,
Hope of mankind, with whom peace is a passion, marches on.
In his trail, glory pursues him wherever he goes.

# XII
# The Unknown Face

I have been for a long time awake in endless quest of the unknown face.
When I saw first the light of the world, I saw its shadow in my mother's face.
When I learnt first to distinguish a man from a man, I saw its image in my father's face.
When I caught first a hand for being able to walk, I saw its sight in my brother's face.
When I became first a little big boy, I saw its meaning in my own friend's face.
When I felt the flutter of my unborn love, I though I would find the unknown face.
When I first glanced at my new-born babe, I thought here was the unknown face.
Ever long since when I was born, my heart has chased the unknown face.
But is there one, of any one, who resembles the face of that unknown face?

Before the birth of my present life, before I saw the light of the day;
Before the birth of my unknown dreams, before I saw this beautiful world,
From the unreached depths of eternity, had been impressed a picture on my lonely heart,
Carried secretly as a treasured longing, always to be traced and always to be chased;
The endless quest of that unknown face.

When I first learnt the alphabets of my mother tongue;

When I first learnt to make one complete sentence;
When I first learnt the lesson how to count;
When I first learnt the method how to differentiate;
Before I learnt to distinguish between falsehood and truth;
Before I came to realize that knowledge had no end
And before I composed my own little poem,
My quest had grown, my heart been ablaze,
I had been afire with the longing for that unknown face.

As I drive along the large and many multi-cornered paths;
As I drive along the labyrinths of Delhi's many-sided ways;
As I look at the ever new and changing faces of women and men,
It is all in quest of that unknown face.

Sometimes I do catch a glimpse, I do make a meaning, I do feel a strength;
Sometimes I do perceive a thrill, I do get a chance, I do have an intuition;
Sometimes I do get an impression that my discovery is just at hand,
But then the subtle airy thing that was born is just lost away.
I am then left puzzled at the loss of the treasured thing,
The loss of that unknown, unknown face.

As I stand alone on the large bank of this river of life
As I make a quest and as I hotly pursue my search,
There appears sometimes some semblance of that unknown face:
In the flowery freshness of a newly born babe,
In the meaningful coyness of a bride just ready to wed,

In the sense of accomplishment of a great discoverer,
In the natural outpourings of a great poet,
In the resounding echoes of an enthralling speech,
In the ideal blend of colours in a really great painting,
In anything and everything when a man achieves something,
But everywhere, after sometime the face loses its shape,
And the face resembling the unknown face
Again becomes the unknown unknown face.

Has any one ever seen the unknown face?

## XIII

# *Has anyone got the answers and does anyone fully know?*

Has any one got the answers and does any one fully know?
What is that which pervades the universe that a man cannot see?
What is that which runs the universe that he himself cannot perceive?
What is that which takes the universe to its set and destined course?
Has any one got the answers and does any one fully know?

Why is it that in life's smooth journey such questions at all arise?
Why is it that many want their answers and what does this signify?
What is there a man must know that he himself cannot see?
And what is the omnipotent spirit of the universe that he must himself feel?

What disturbs the peace of his mind when his heart is locked in someone's sight?
What shakes the balance of his mind when a dear one is in serious plight?
What elates him to many dizzy heights when his heart meets its own delight?
Who has got their answers and who has got the know?

What wakes in him pious feelings and deep longings for eternity?
What inspires him to seek new visions, mental peace and serenity?
Why does he seek routes longer when short ones could serve his ends?
Why does he prefer truth when falsehood caused no offence?

Why does he give up his own happiness and feel sad on seeing others in pain?
Why does he seek mind's own balance and often ignore what is just in vain?
Why does he get tired and impatient when he could have been a little quiet?
Why does he get ready to die for others when his cause his attention invites?

Why does he gamble and take chances with a short and mortal life?
When life could be spent without any risk and free of any strife.
What leads him to leave his hearth and home and what carries him far and far?
He could be at peace in his own little home and be unknown to one and all.

Has any one got the answers and does any one fully know?

## XIV

## *I write today of the conception, what is truth?*

I write today of the conception, what is truth?
I think today of the time when man first saw truth.
I think today of man who first saw truth.
In the remote dark times man who had to grope his way,
When he first arrived in this world, and stood face to face
With future about which no one born before had any taste.
Then he was the first to see the light of the day.
That day he saw the world with a virgin mind;
The first impact awakened in him yearnings to know more.
That is how was conceived curiosity,
And that is how was born truth.

Every time till today, the same way
No sooner one is born
Than one starts one's journey of curiosity,
Than one starts one's pursuit of truth.

Curiosity is born with man; truth is born with man.
He must know what he is; he must know what the world is.
Thus he seeks to know everything; thus he seeks to realise everything.
With the birth of the world was born truth, but it was concealed in man's ignorance.
The awakening of his mind helps to remove the veil over truth.
Always in the world truth prevailed and still prevails.

For ever till the world exists truth will ever prevail.
Has not every one himself to discover truth?
Has he not himself to practise truth?
And has he not himself to experience truth?
Truth only comes personally to every one.
It does not come without seeking to any one.

Any one who seeks truth must strive for it.
Any one who wants to be true must try for it.
All that we believe to be true is what we are told to be true.
All that we know as truth is what we have found as truth.
At every stage of one's life one is getting a taste of truth.
No one has ever realised truth without ever trying for it.
Man has to overcome his ignorance to come near truth.
Man must get enlightened to know what is truth.
One who gets enlightened knows a great deal of truth.

The journey of humanity for discovery of truth was never smooth.
It was verily a journey of climbing a steep hill.
It was not a march through straight and clear roads,
But more a march through circuitous and difficult routes,
Where humanity met steep heights and deep falls.
Having had to overcome rivers in fury of floods,
Having had to cross deserts blinded by violent storms,
It also came across in its journey great oasis of calm.
It also passed through periods of rare glory
When it discovered any truth.
Though sadly the entire journey was punctuated with many wars;
Though humanity sank low when it turned against truth,
But humanity has continued to trudge on its journey
In one relentless search of truth.
Humanity has experimented with many forms of living,

And with many types of government.
Humanity has discovered forms of art and types of religion.
All its search, all its research and all its march
Was to find out a way to curb man's base traits;
Was to curb those animal instincts that give him not any peace;
Was to find a way out to strive for a mental peace and physical ease;
And a method to live together without any mutual strife or enmity,
And to ultimately discover the final truth.

Is he still anywhere near the bliss that he sought?
Is he still anywhere in sight of his goal?
Is he still not like a being, having lost his moorings?
Is he still near the stage where he could see only truth?
What is this conflict between his strive for truth and animal traits?
Why does he want to establish kingdom of truth through use of sword?
Why does his truth fear the truth of any other one?
Why does he conceive his own truth as the final one?
Why does he not look upon truth as infinite?
Why does he not conceive it as if without any end?
Why is mankind steeped in ignorance and bathed in prejudice?
Wearing heavily the fetters of bigotry,
Confining itself to the cocoons of narrow mindedness,
And not come out in the bright sunshine of truth.

Is not truth bigger than the world?
Is not truth larger than the universe?
Does it not include all the planets and the stars?
Does it not include everything, we know not?

How much do we know of truth that we war over it?
How little do we know of it that we make claims for it?

Truth was born with the world and has for ever prevailed in the world.
Truth is what is final, though man knows not what is the final truth.
Truth is the supreme force that determines the course of the universe.
Truth is what prevails when everything else fails.
Every religion, every philosophy, every cult and every viewpoint
Is at best an attempt to know what is true,
But never can replace what is finally true.

Truth will survive though we will all die.
Truth ever lives and will never die,
Though mankind may live or die.

But why do we often talk as if we alone knew truth?
Why do we often hate those whose views we do not appreciate?
Why do we not understand the various facets of truth?
The entire history of mankind is a long chronicle of labours
For its constant search for truth.
Cannot we open its pages and read
That many new views and creeds were put before the world?
This appeared to all, who preached their doctrines,
As the final word in truth.
The many philosophies, the many religions, the many views and thoughts
That fill the pages of history and that claimed many followers,

Are in many respects consigned to old records.
What remains is the shell, the pearl having slipped away,
And we remain busy loving the shape of the shell.
We show the world the shell enlarged as an idol;
We remember the outer form and are oblivious of what has slipped away.

The lopsided emphasis on many a ritual,
The superficial aspect of many a viewpoint
Has been often put forward with great stress.
Even truth is often presented as a slogan.
Even truth is often used to achieve a falsehood.
Truth is often the first casualty in a war.
Thus truth has met many accidents in its journey towards progress;
It had to halt so often and compromise with falsehood.
But ultimately truth remained truth and falsehood, falsehood.
Even today the world is divided in two different camps,
And each camp claims right on its side.
Each camp tries to find out examples to support its view.
Each camp twists facts to prove its claims.
Each camp forgets the world was often split in two viewpoints,
Two philosophies, two sets of arguments, and the two ways of life;
And each side thought that in clash will survive its truth.
Neither the men who clashed nor the truth they fought for, survives today.
Even today, men look zealous, convinced that truth is on their side.
Even today, men are prepared to stake everything;
They imagine they can halt the march of time.
They think they can force the truth to obey their commands.

They tell the world to only believe in their brand of truth.
But the men who conceive the truth are only mortal men,
And no one who is born can be a perfect one.
They may have been wiser men, and even God's chosen ones,
But no one who bears the mortal frame can escape its limitations.
The eyes of men see only what is in the reach of their eyes;
Their thinking is circumscribed by what they know at all.
It is after all only men who conceive their truth.
How can they make that truth bigger than their mortal form?
How can they make truth immortal with their own perception?
How can they call anything final when truth is infinite?
How can they give truth a brighter light than they themselves possess?
How can they thus override the final form of truth?

Every time men stand on the brink of war
For the sake of their truthful side,
They little realize that the opposite side
Is as much seized of its righteousness.
How can mortal men decide which is the truthful side?
How can they decide that truth is on their side?
Why should they be the judge as to what is the final truth?
Should, therefore, the march of such men be not halted?
Selfish men who take the world to the brink of war;
Selfish men who, to conceal the weaknesses of their side, take to sword;
Such selfish men only thwart the progress of truth.
For one, who has the final truth on his side,
Requires support of nothing else but truth alone,
As truth is the most potent weapon invented so far.

# XV
# This Frame of Flesh

I often wonder about this frame of flesh,
Held together by bones and blood,
Kept alive by a strange mystery,
Strutting as humans in this world.
All these forms move in their individuality.
All bear their own special personality.
Not one is like the other,
But all of them move in their frames of flesh.
So are beings from sub-human class:
The vast class of mammals, birds and other reptiles,
All possess their special frames.
But how different is the human frame:
Setting civilizations and founding kingdoms,
Making peace and waging wars,
Making new discoveries and finding new paths,
And even trying to transcend beyond human thought;
Further advancing many new theories,
And laying basis of many new thoughts.

The moment one is born, start strong throbbings of heart,
The heart that beats and beats every moment.
Does any one know why beats the heart?
The heart that lets man live every moment.
Heart is the engine that keeps this frame.
Heart is the primum mobile of this life.
As long as the heart pulsates the frame is called alive.
This frame moves and moves and goes wherever it wants to go.
It does all that, that it wants to do.

It is as free to live as it is free to die.
It is free in its actions, it is free in its life.

Up to what is this frame of flesh?
It has its moods, it has its views.
It sleeps, it wakes, it loves and hates.
It is full of ambitions, it is full of grit.
It is full of fear, it is full of cowardice.
The limitation is of the frame of flesh;
The weakness is of the frame of flesh;
The strength is of the strange subtlety
That is not seen but is often felt.
Its energy is the unknown mystery
That pervades whether one is lean or fat.

This frame of flesh moves from place to place,
From town to town, from land to sea,
On land, in air, and at high seas,
Beyond the limitations of this earth in outer space,
Dashing across high hills and deep dales,
Overcoming handicaps of nature, and barriers of ignorance,
Prepared for serious risks, and ready for new adventures,
Seized by yearnings of an unknown mystery,
This frame of flesh is a strange machinery.

All the frames all over the world
Are in tune with frames all over the world.
Frame calls a frame, and together they make friendly frames.
Why they like each other depends on the shape of their frames.
Those whose flesh is harmoniously cast make beautiful frames.
But some whose flesh is cast in irregular shapes make

ugly frames.

Some are taken to each other by the quality of shapes,
While some are influenced by the colour of flesh on frames.
Some think that the colour of flesh is not material to the quality of frames,
And what is essential is the inner strength, not the form of frame.
Still most women and men choose their mates depending on what they prefer in shapes.
Some preferring mellowed shapes, others wanting stronger frames.
It is the contour of frames that makes women and men together one,
That brings about a union strong and everlasting one.
There are frames that look lovelier than other frames.
There are frames that look stronger than other frames.
The frames that look lovelier and stronger do so
By what they inherit from other frames,
As also how frames are shaped and flesh is tended
And by what they get from other frames.

These frames made of flesh, bones and blood
Reflect the state of mind of every one.
Some whose minds are happy and gay
Show their frames in a poised and healthy state.
Where sorrow and grief overwhelm the minds of men,
The frames and shapes display the same portends.
Where minds draw a blank from their surrounding state,
The frames of flesh show the same expression on their empty face.

It is frames that are held together by bonds of love.
It is frames that are held apart by razor of hate.

Why some frames love, and why some frames hate,
Why those in love are led to hate,
Why those in hate decide to love,
Is not known either to one or the other frame.
But frames overflow with views, and their views always change.

Thus frames full of love and hate and views move,
And they appear to move leaving endless grooves.
These frames of flesh make patterns endless as they move,
And their movements show the viewpoint followed by them.

These frames of flesh move across the world,
Short-lived, conceited, emphemeral, temporal,
Full of pride on their achievements, conditioned by their past,
Quarreling with their present and hopeful of their future.

Mankind has spent its life in trying to understand the frames.
What makes them love, what makes them hate?
How they live and how they behave?
No one is yet wiser about the why and how of these frames.
What we know about the why and how of frames
Is what we presume and what we assume.
What we know, we accept as true,
And what is left unknown, we presume to be true.
We cannot explain the why and how of life.
We can only see the present state of life.
We can present the state of life in symbols of something
As we present symbols in a dance beautiful and elating.
Nothing is captured in words, but we say, here is harmony.
We say here are gestures that convey the meaning of life.

Thus what we know not, we try to understand through gestures in life.
In this way we explain the why and how of life.
We believe in abstractions built on suppositions.
We explain not objectively the warp and woof of life,
Because no one knows surely the reason of start of life.

Does any one know about the origin of the first frame?
No one has met one who saw the first frame.
All these frames appear to have come from some other frames,
And what we see as mass of men are the product of so many frames.
These frames arrive and these frames depart.
They appear to come and go as eternal travellers.
Can any one ever explain what happens to one when one dies?
Or is there any one who has the memory of his past life?
We only see the frame of flesh so long as it lasts,
And when we see it not, we say the man has passed.

So long as there is breath in this human garb,
There is life in ever-throbbing and restless heart.
There is also the constant questioning heart enquiring, "Who am I"?
And 'I' wanting to know from frame "Who you are?"
Some unknown mystery always occupies the heart,
Often leading to conflict between 'I' inside, and flesh in cast.
The flesh says, "Obey me, I am your Master, my heart."
"While 'I' says, "Fool, you are merely born to die at last.
"I am the invisible 'I' sitting in every frame.
"The 'I' that is not a part of flesh and frame.
"It is that 'I' that ever remains alive
"Whatever may happen to flesh or frame cast to die."

Flesh says "No one is sure where 'I' goes,
"Whether it disappears with the frame of flesh
"When everything to nothingness goes.
"As you are never seen, you are what you are—
"A mere invisible pretender."
These two always try to dominate and stress their part.
They remain at war and we know not which is true—
The 'I' that sits like the master in this frame of flesh,
Or the frame that disobeys 'I' and remains true to flesh.

There are some who to resolve this conflict,
To know what unknown voice ever haunts the mind,
What unseen power carries it to journey's end,
Are often ready to consume the frame;
Are often ready to burn the frame.
They cause it intense pain,
Subjecting it to deep sufferings,
Putting it to cruel tests,
Thinking such a course will purify the frame,
Imagining such trials will make it behave,
Believing such methods will condition the frame,
And make 'I' much stronger than the frame.
It has been a difficult task for 'I' to defeat the frame,
Because frame knows 'I' sits caged in the frame,
And what can 'I' do so long flesh remains flesh, and frame, frame.
Only when flesh will cease to be flesh and frame frame,
That 'I' will be released from its cage,
Then 'I' will merge in other 'I' and remain in endless search
Till it gets caged in another frame.

The frame of flesh ever moves carrying the questioning 'I',
And always trying to understand what wants this 'I'.
Inside the human frame sits 'I' like an ever-burning flame,

Leaving the man in endless quest about this meaning of flame.
Flame wants to overpower flesh and show what it is.
But flesh and frame stand as obstinate handicaps preventing its working.
Flesh says, "Flesh is flesh and frame is frame.
"How can flame overcome so easily flesh and frame."
Flame says, "I am the light, I am the guide, oh, flesh and frame."
But frame and flesh listen not, so thick is flesh on frame.
Those who feel not the strength of flame remain true to flesh,
And flesh grows over flesh and we see massive frames.
When flame feels choked with massive walls of flesh,
It heats the flesh and seeks from it an outlet.
Then we see flame awaken flesh from its yawning sleep,
And flesh wanting to shed its heavy and fettering fatigue.
Then flesh opens its eyes and sees a new light,
And between frame of flesh and flame starts the eternal fight.

Flesh has often been at war with flame inside
Whose command it often ignores,
And often it follows its own course.
Often it goes on its own way;
Often it evolves peculiar methods.
Often it thinks flame not as important as the frame.
Often it imagines frame could exist without the flame.
But flame must burn if frame is to remain alive.
So flame flickers and fights to call the frame to rise,
And when the two agree not
Flame puts up its fight.
But often frame puts down the murmurings of flame.
Frame tells flame not to interfere in its game.
Frame wants to function in its own way.

Frame wants flame to be put away.
Then frame exists devoid of the grace of flame,
Then frame tries to show flesh's true qualities,
And flesh stands in all its terrible tragedy.
Thus we see the specimens of unbalanced minds.
We see men turn to anger and hate.
We see men become cruel, barbaric ones.
We see men become veritable satans.
We see men cause havoc and confusion.
Blood boils in such frames and passions have their sway,
And we see how men display their base traits.
Flame sees the game of flesh in all its naked shame,
But is powerless before the cruel sight of heartless frame.

But lo! Flame is eternal and not frame.
It refuses to keep quiet even though frame wants it to keep quiet
In the quality of flame it is determined to fight.
No one has ever extinguished this flame,
And there remains this flame ever alive.
Flame is a part of the invisible entire flame,
Illuminating the life in every frame.
Flame is the light through which each one can see.
Flame is the flutter that stands for heart's throb and beat.
Flame is the master of frame guiding it to go ahead.
Flame helps to see clearly the right path ahead.
Flame always advises men to remain on the truthful side.
Flame is more powerful than anything that lives in frame.
It has its special way of responding to the call of other flames.
It has its unique method of getting in touch with other flames.
Flame often shows its working in frames of all types.
It often shows how flame is the eternal force alive,
And how it triumphs against heavy odds in the end of life.

Do we not see base men turn into great spiritual giants?
Men in abject hate, make absolute love;
Men return to reason, having lost their way.
We see models of clay turn into pillars of strength;
All the work of flame illuminating everything.

When, however, flesh calls the other flesh,
When it cannot resist the call of other flesh;
When it decides to merge in the other flesh;
All the inhibitions that tied down the frame;
All his resolutions, all his decisions
Are thrown away merging flesh in flesh.
Unless conditioned strongly by the flame,
The quality of flesh remains as that of flesh.
Flesh always merges in the other's flesh.
Flesh is always warring against its inner self;
Flesh is ever trying to score over the strength of flame.
The game of flesh that wages war against its inner self
Is as old as human frame.
No one has been ever born who could fully master flesh,
Otherwise how could he be in flesh and frame?

The game of life is the game of flesh,
Because men exist and move in their frames of flesh.
So long as men live, they live in their frame of flesh.
No one in this cast of flesh can escape the game of flesh,
For, all have to function through their own frames of flesh.
What we labour to earn we do for the sake of flesh.
What we choose to eat we do for raising the fat on flesh.
We are busy every moment in maintaining the health of flesh,
And are ever concerned at any threat to the state of flesh.
For the large increasing number of women and men,
It is flesh and flesh and it is flesh and flesh.

We ever come in the world from the state of one flesh
And ever move on to join the state of other flesh.
We ever arrive in flesh and we ever depart from flesh.
Through the strength of flesh and from the glory of flesh,
Our journey starts in flesh and our life ends in flesh.
We see the large world move, seized by the craze of flesh,
Seized by the worries of flesh
And burdened by the problems of flesh.
How would the mounting number of frames find food to eat?
How would flesh over flesh ever find place to live?
How would the naked flesh ever find clothes to wear?
And how would the angry frames ever find peace to exist?
These frames of flesh ushered by the game of flesh
Are ever living for their own individual game of flesh.
To deliver more flesh and to leave their flesh in flesh,
And to die in flesh and to be born again in flesh.
The world is ever busy in increasing the strength of flesh.
Women are ever trying to decorate and beautify their flesh.
Men are ever trying to be youthful in their frame of flesh.
They both are set to the same strength of opposing currents,
Having for each other a strong and sudden attraction.
The call of one flesh to other flesh makes two persons one,
Holding women and men in strong invisible bonds.
But flesh for ever has not the same stamina and strength.
Flesh is being born to grow, stay and then decay.
But think women and men that flesh would remain ever young.
Both are seized by the mirage of looking ever young.
They adopt artificial means to perpetuate the strength of flesh,
And ever wish to cling to this deception.
Flesh for ever does not remain young.
Flesh can never be the same ever strong.

Flesh wears itself out every moment,
And in everyone's life a time comes
When flesh fails to respond to the call of flesh.
When mind orders, but flesh replies "Now, I am gone."
Then women and men feel the terrible waste of flesh.
Either they evolve new ways to strengthen the fire of flesh,
Or get in touch with their flame to make up for the cold of flesh.
But so long as flesh could answer the call of flesh,
Flesh was busy in its engagements with other flesh;
Flesh felt no need to call for the aid of flame.
But when flesh ceased to be useful as a flesh,
It cried in despair for the aid of flame.

Does anyone know what invites flesh to flesh?
Is it the strength of flesh that invites the other flesh?
Or is it the powerful flame which invites the other flame.
Flame radiates in its person a unique, magic charm,
Which transcends imperfections of flesh,
And handicaps of frame.
There is a limit beyond which flesh does not count
And only flame remains.
Whatever be the cause of one flesh inviting another flesh,
Whether flame or flesh, one or together of them,
The world remains at peace till they are together one.
But when flesh hates the other flesh,
Or the fighting flame disturbs the balance of flesh,
And frame listens not to flame,
Then frames become veritable fiends out to drink each other's blood.

Then frames fight frames,
And then men count the slaughtered frames.
That is the fate that frames face
When frames of flesh are at war with themselves.

How can frame be at peace with flame inside?
The problem has staggered civilization since its inception.
The question has begged an answer since man was born.
Man has evolved many theories and endless viewpoints.
Man has often erased himself to realize life's meaning.
Man has slain other men to extend his dominions.
Countless men have spent their lives and failed in their mission
To understand the cause of their having been born,
And to know the reason of their existence.
The conflict has remained eternal since man was born.
The quest has pursued him wherever he has gone.
Flame has remained for man an unsolved riddle
And led frame of flesh to take repeated births,
But still failed to arrive at any solution,
Making man himself an unsolved puzzle.
This is the quest that man has for ever faced
And has failed to find an answer of his misgivings.

We see on the one hand frames appearing fit and strong,
Prepared to face the world and ready for any action.
Then frames think how can there be another bliss in life,
If man has all the comforts, health and money;
If man has all the luck to favour him;
If flesh and frame remain in harmony with the world wide,
How else does frame in flesh wish to be satisfied?
On the other hand we see men in confused and dispirited state.
We see them in tatters and reduced to skeletons.
We see them lying low and left in a broken state.
There, flesh is ever begging frames to rise.
Such frames move about devoid of any flesh;
The world displeased with these frames in poor flesh.

Misery, sorrow and poverty are the mates of such frames,
And death devours the haste and hurry of these frames.
Still, there are kinds of frames with flesh of different types.
One, where flesh is rich and insulated to misfortunes of life.
The other, where flesh is coarse and revengeful to smooth course of life.
But there is still another type,
Where flesh is sensitive to murmurings of flame inside,
And is ever seeking a proper meaning of life.
Frames of various types are not ever seeking a meaning of life
Because no frame of flesh is ever the same at all ages of life.
It is changing every minute under new phases of life.
What it did yesterday, it might not do today.
What it thought yesterday, it might not think today.
It seeks not always the aid of ever burning flame
If it is not in conflict with life's daily strain.
Frame of flesh is ever seeking favours of fortune,
And is ever hopeful of being bestowed with all its boons.
Where fortune favours a frame of flesh
Flame remains often in great neglect.
But fortune is not an admirer of any chosen frames.
It has its fickle ways of favouring some frames.
For no reason it can give up its past beloved frames,
Picking up some new ones for no cause at all,
And keeping its chosen victims guessing about its part.
When fortune casts off its previous shell and seeks a new shelter,
It is the turn of flame to have its laugh,
And chide the frame of flesh for purposeless past.
Flame knows how flesh is in aimless pursuits.
It knows very well the game of fickle fortune.
It has been a resident of all types of human frames.

It also knows that frames follow a path,
Set in a circuitous routes, full of high altitudes and serious pitfalls.
Therefore, flame keeps up its constant fight.
It calls upon the frame of flesh to mind the fickleness of life.
It often says, "I am your Master, I am your Lord.
"And now it is my turn to assert my part."

In every frame, flame tries to create a responsive echo,
No matter flesh is more or less, soft or hard.
In all those frames where flame gets a favourable echo
It gives them peace and peeps out in a halo,
Presenting such frames as specimens of its perfect art.
In all types of frames, flame is in permanent existence
And men benefit from it as they deserve its grace.
If they try to shut out its part, it gives them not its blessings,
Leaving these frames in misery of their misfortunes.
While those who believe in the immortality of flame;
Those who have faith in the final power of flame;
And those who see that flame alone gives peace,
Not fortunes attendant on frame,
Spend their life in constant quest of flame.
By studying its qualities, by understanding its efficacies
And by being absorbed in its ecstasies,
They ever seek to be in communion with flame.

Every being has flame as its permanent resident.
Every one now and then feels the presence of this companion.
Every one has his periods of quests
When flame wakes up a frame for its quest.
It is flame alone that wakes up a frame for its quest,
Leading the frame in quest of flame, and flame in quest of

other flames.

Is it quest alone that determines a man's future?
Or is there any other overpowering purpose
That brings a man to the world through cycle of births?
Man is a torch in which burns a flame,
The torch ever taken over by coming generations.
From an old frame, flame passes on to a new frame,
Leaving old garb of torch in a previous birth.
It is to make flame,
Concealed in the case of flesh,
Visible to other beings
That frames remain in constant quest.
This quest is man's main helper and saviour,
Moving him everyday in his quest of quest.
It is through his thinking that he can pursue his quest,
Using his frame of flesh as his instrument.
He tries to train his frame of flesh to obey his commands,
To temper its traits for smooth living with fellow frames,
To seek a living for preserving the cast of his frame,
And for being able to pursue his quest through his garb of frame.

This frame of flesh is a tiny little thing in the world of living,
But its mind makes it the most extra-ordinary thing.
Mind of man is his best friend and worst enemy,
That can raise him to the rarest glories of ecstasy
Or debase him to the farthest end of a tragedy.
What makes man is his mind,
Leaving its undeveloped state an animal.
It is mind of man that gives the world the essence of its existence;
That treasures memories of past and cherishes dreams of future,

And that gives a meaning to everything that fills the vast universe.
Has not mind in man made the world what it is today?
Has not mind given the world its present shape?
When men have decided to delve deep into nature's mysteries,
Have they not conquered air, space, land and sea?
Has not human mind reached sometimes the zenith of its glory?
Have we not examples of the past when mind of man stood in its rarity?
The mind that thinks is a strange complex thing,
That has gone to build the entire world;
Its culture, civilization, science and its machines.
The history of the world is the history of mind
That interpreted the surroundings that it saw,
And shaped the world by its interpretations.
Often mind thinks that it can best think,
Though the level of thinking at a particular time
Is conditioned by surroundings in which it can think.
Thus mind has met handicaps in pursuit of curiosity,
Created by the level at which a man can think.
Still there are rarer minds whose horizon in thinking
Goes beyond the level that others can see,
And such rare minds ensure the progress of the world
By thinking beyond the conception of the world.
Such thinking men produce countless permutations
That others interpret as they appeal to them,
And as they echo in their minds a kindred spirit.
Often such rare minds come before their times
And men of the time fail to understand what they said at all.
Again what such rare men say at proper time,
Is wrongly interpreted by those who follow them.
Thus the frame of flesh has risen high and gone low,

Corresponding to the chance availed by men who wished to think.
But where the frames of flesh cared not to muse and to think,
They failed to avail of the chance given to them.
Mind makes a man who makes the world,
And when mind unmakes a man he unmakes the world.
Mind is man's precursor and carrier, helper and pride;
His dignity, beauty, his hope and his eyes.
Mind can destroy what is noble and good in life,
As also obliterate from this world traces of its own life.
It is mind that helps man to examine his schemes of life,
As also thwarts and puts a stop to all his plans of life.
A man has to attune his mind to obey his commands
Or loses himself in abject surrender to life's confusions.

Mind pursues the path that it can ever see,
But can never be the judge of its own working.
Thus mind goes ahead and undertakes its tasks,
Knowing little that it may be sowing seeds of its own loss.
Mind may be a mighty thing, but it is blind without a compass.
Mind may have achieved anything, but it is useless without a purpose.
If mind exists without a creative cause,
If it fails to find an echo in life's purpose;
If it is sustained not by the strength of flame;
If it gets not light from its own illumination,
It carries not a frame of flesh very far.
It brings about a sad end to all its tasks.
A mind nurtured not by the strength of flame,
Is like a cast in frame of flesh without any aim.

Mind exists as a part of a frame of flesh,

Present in the invisibility of its existence.
It guides the destinies of those that it dictates
From the thinking produced by this strange apparatus.
When flame burns strongly in a frame,
Mind is the first to see the change.
Flame beams its rays to the mind
And where mind is sensitive it lets in the light.
The rays of flame give mind a broad and new conception,
Helping man to see the world in a different light.
For mind the world assumes a new shape,
Where enmities take to heels, hates evaporate,
And where compassion, love and grace are born.
But mind has a varying level at different periods of life;
Always it cannot judge the strength of flame at every turn of life.
Always it cannot see how strong is the illumination,
And always it cannot be blessed by the grace of flame.
For this the mind must remove from it the veil of ignorance,
Mind must shed the darkness enveloping it,
And see how bright is the illumination
When veil of cloud is lifted from its thinking.
It is through his mind that man can see his illumination,
For mind has to receive its nourishment for its task.
When mind has opened its windows to let in the light,
That light is for ever worn by the frame of flesh.
Those who close their windows to the light of flame
Are lost in the jungle of their own confusion.
Where flame shines brightly in a human frame,
It illuminates the entire universe.
The light shed by such a flame awakens other flames,
And calls other frames to rise to its response.
We see the miracles that such flames perform
When they awaken the conscience of the universe.
Like this is born bliss ushered by one

Whose flame illuminates all and everything.
Men mortal ever sit in endless wait
For the grace of such blessed men
Whose presence thus for ever shows
How immortal is the light illumining everything.
And how every one is bound by that invisible spirit
That lives in each one of us.
It is for that vision that is rarely seen
That men go in search from place to place;
That they visit many centres of pilgrimage,
Made divine by association of such rare souls.
Thus the spirit, that had awakened in the life of chosen ones,
Is still felt at every place they had ever graced,
And even stones get hallowed in human eye,
Because the spirit shining there had consecrated them.

What else does mind do
When it has a work to do?
It carries the task it has to do,
And puts it before the powerful flame.
Flame examines the viewpoint placed by mind
And conveys its advice to the frame.
If frame follows the advice offered by flame,
And does its task as approved by flame,
It makes light the task executed by frame,
Leaving the doer in a tranquil and blessed state.
Where a course is followed not as advised by flame,
And doer cuts off light offered by flame,
He performs his task without the light of flame.
He can see not the way he should have gone.
He loses the path he was going before.
He goes on his way completely alone.
He then lands himself in a chaos of confusion.
He is pushed about by forces let loose by him.

He goes to an end different from what was chosen.
He little knew how for every cause there is an effect,
And for every effect there is a cause.
There is never any effect without a cause
And never any cause without a previous cause.
As he had followed not advice offered by flame,
What he did, led him to a different end.
What he had aimed at he could never achieve,
For there was no return from the place where he had gone.
He had followed a course which displaced his approach.
He was knocked about by events over which he had no control.


He had followed his path without the light of flame
And he could reach never the aim and end of his goal.
He was like a lost soul following an unknown course
Without a rudder in the sea of life.
Caught in the storm he met his end,
When tide had turned against his course.
Mind dares reject advice of flame at its own pain,
For the frame would be led to a sad and an ignoble end.
When mind takes to a path shut from ever-advising flame,
It is on being misled to a course of quick returns.
That course shows at hand an immediate gain,
Tempting to grasp the end so suddenly seen.
The path shown by flame is a narrow one,
And the goal seen at end is at a distant place,
Requiring the seeker to walk in a straight way,
Without any side-glances of greedy eyes;
Without any stop for a look at its side-shows,
For one may fall in any opening on any side.
Once having lost track of advice offered by flame,
The frame will be led to a life of desultoriness;

Where confusion will abound;
Where objectivity will be lost;
Where men will cut one another by acts of betrayal;
Where men will defeat one another in cleverness;
Where immediate ends will overshadow one's final gains.
To see the beacon light shown by our flame
May our actions be attuned to the temper of flame,
And run not counter to its qualities.
May our daily life correspond with the permanent flame
And wait for its considered replies.
May our thoughts arise from the fountain of mind,
Powered by the boundless flame.
May our mind seek to be in tune with the eternal flame,
And keep it before its observant eyes,
And fail not even once to be without its aid.
May the fat of flesh be not allowed to blur the keen vigil,
Kept by flame as one's conscience,
And may mind be ever inspired by the eternal flame,
Lighting one's vision.

How can mind broaden its vision in its journey of life?
How can it shed flesh's passions that cloud its judgment?
How can it acquire a composure for further enlightenment?
This is a perplexity faced by man in his quest,
And if it is not solved, it stops his quest.
In his quest to understand the mystery of flame
May man borrow from flame some of its light,
And use that light to broaden his conception,
Raising higher and higher his level of thinking.
Flame could lend more light to repeat the process
Till both are set to the same response.
Until that stage is reached, frames of flesh would move,
Borrowing every time a little from the light of flame.
When mind has raised high its level of thinking;

When it has acquired its own independent strength,
It could return the light to the flame borrowed from it.
Thus a stage is reached when mind would only see
Light shed by flames in other beings.
Then flesh becomes weak to assert itself
In all pervading strength released by flame.
May mind ever see through the light of flame
And be denied not the guidance to be followed by it.

There are two mirrors of mind in this human frame:
One that reflects images of the world outside,
The other reflecting images of the hidden side.
The one exposed to the images of the world outside,
Stores its treasures in safe corners of memory.
The hidden side being left to receive such images
That are found unfit to be stored by memory.
The sub-conscious self is the hidden side
Meant to absorb the shocks of life,
Where such aspirations and frustrations find their way
As could not be attuned to the trends of time,
Being far removed from realities.
The two sides of mirror perform their tasks,
Holding themselves ever in an even balance.
Whenever there is a jolt in the balance of these mirrors,
Created by a sudden shake-up of mind,
Images get distorted and men feel just lost.
There are angles at which such mirrors are held,
Determining the manner they reflect their thoughts.
Those whose reflections arise from an harmonious angle,
Give out many profound and meaningful thoughts.
Artists are those whose mirrors of mind are placed
At an angle where they reflect only beautiful thoughts.
They touch a chord in their mind that is also in tune
With the spirit pervading the universe.
There are men whose angles of mirrors are secured at

their ends,
And such men feel secured till the time of their end.
While those whose angles of mirrors are removed from their ends,
Become nervous wrecks and lose their entire balance.
A balance is required in the poise of the mirror,
Otherwise poise sought by man is completely lost.
There is a balance that the two sides of mirror strike
With each other's side,
And that makes man mind's own and true reflection.
Every action that we ever do;
Every thought that we ever perceive;
Every view that we ever express;
Everything that we see others do;
Everything that ever happens in the world;
All leave their images on the two sides of mind.
We always need to be in harmony;
We must not do anything that brings us in conflict
With mirror's two sides,
And these should ever balance evenly,
The balance that in turn is to be ever attuned
To the illumination pervading every being.


This frame of flesh has two sides of life,
The life of flesh, of bones and blood
That we see walking and moving, waking and sleeping;
The side that puts the world of animals at par with him.
There is the other side, the composition of his thoughts and yearnings,
Arising from harmony of his conscious and sub-conscious self,
And from flame illuminating and widening his thinking,
That gives him grace, form and beauty,
And determines how much he has risen over others of

his race.
It is that side that keeps him awake when it is time to sleep;
That helps him to see what is not in others' reach;
That awakes in him sense of love and compassion,
Consideration and discrimination,
That goes to draw contours of his sense of appreciation;
That shows the broad basis of his personality,
And that distinguishes his culture from that of others.
This frame of flesh has boundless potential of strength,
For the entire chronicle of romance of human mind
Is but a tribute to the side that lifts men from the lowest rung
To the display and consummation of those shining qualities
That could put to shame even the brightest sun.
Thus there are born among women and men,
Such women and men as bear like others their frames of flesh,
Moving and living as all other men and women do,
But who live outside their frames of flesh.
Such souls master the strength of their flesh
And make their bodies instruments
To perpetuate the glory of the eternal flame.
It is such men as feel convinced
That life of flesh often blurs their vision;
That flesh stands in the way of their spiritual awakening.
Thus they subordinate flesh to their own existence.
They raise high the life of their spiritual strength.
They control the hunger of their physical frame.
They sublimate flesh to a new response,
And their flesh ceases to disturb their spiritual life.
There have been men who left their life of flesh
And stood apart as Buddha, Christ and Gandhi did.
They tamed their flesh, and saw beyond its limitations

The life of the world in its true perspective.
They saw flesh as a delusion that blinded men,
That led them to pursuits aimless and ignoble,
Forsaking the tasks they should have performed.
These noble men placed before the world two sides of life:
The life of physical side leading men to hate and love,
Making men of flesh fight and remain in perpetual fright,
And unconcerned of what would happen when death would strike.
These great men showed that there was the other side that never died,
That gave a meaning to the life of every one,
And that gave this world the immortality of its existence.
These men showed that living was made not by violent calls of flesh
But by love, compassion, understanding and kindness.
These men did what they ever said.
They lived up to what they ever preached.
They achieved what other men in flesh could not reach.
They showed flesh was weak before their powerful strength.
They showed that not flesh, but their spirit was the real strength.
They achieved an ecstasy that men had ever aspired to reach,
And thus they held masses of men in their spell.
They reached the minds of men by the rare vision they possessed,
Stirring the dormant flame in those where it lay quiet.
The dormant flame shaken, shot to a strong brilliance,
Awakening men to see the glow enveloping them.
The paths lighted by these rare men are still trodden by all,
Making the journey a blessing for those who follow

them.
The names of rare men are ever enshrined
In the hearts of those succeeding them.
For the flame that burned in them is still aflame,
Awakening the flame in us to their response.
These great ones bound the world by strings of their thoughts.
They made the world one by the strength of their ideas.
These men of light always challenged flesh,
And left legacy of the challenge to those who followed them.
They themselves achieved the immortality that they showed.
They showed what man could achieve through strength of love.
They proved how compassion ruled the hearts of men,
How love was the only bond that held the world as one,
And how love was the world's moving force alone,
And man its boundless potential.
Has man not loved other male and female frames?
And loved the women and men of many a tale.
Has he not loved insects, animals and birds of the world?
Nay, he has often loved everything of the universe.
It is in its love that frame of flesh has stood in its glory.
It is in its love that frame of flesh has showed its beauty.
It is in its love that frame of flesh has been loved.
It is in its love that the world has stood the test of eternity.
It is in its love that the past is respected and ever inspires.
It is in its love that one awaits future with hope and tenderness.

Love is what makes a man,
And what is left is naught.
But when this frame of flesh burns with anger and hate;
When an iron curtain is drawn on its invisible mind;

When nothing can pierce its mysterious walls;
When nothing but scorching bitterness further inflames the insatiable revenge,
Then one knows not what unknown evil seizes the spirit of man,
And drives it to its doom.
Then nothing, no sacrifice and no propitiation can be of any avail;
Then this frame of flesh can become more ugly than any animal.
It looks as if the array of frames, bearing semblance to human beings,
Has brought the world near its end,
And disturbed the balance of the entire world.
Then minds of men go to sleep
And the phase that showed vision of great ecstasy and beauty,
Is all gone, replaced by demons and evil-looking men
Who live as fiends carrying hearts full of fire of revenge.
When this comes about then such frames of flesh become terrors
As cruelty and barbarism only satisfy,
And the entire glory, beauty, and greatness of human frame is cast to dust.

At every cross-road of world's history, compassion and love have stood as signposts,
Pointing the way to the world to be followed by it.
At every stage when the world had been threatened with extinction;
When hatred had had its sway,
And terror and fright had seized the minds of men,
Compassion and love appeared as saviours of men,
Incarnating themselves in some rare men,
Representing at best the world's creative urge.

It is specimen of such men who always save the world,
By calling a halt to man's destructive traits,
And seek a response in the flame of every man.
Such men help to brighten the flame of every one,
And uplift the vast mass of humans to a new vision,
To bring about a change in the life of the world.
How noble and sincere are the mass of men,
And how far have they risen to the call of new message,
Depends upon the strength of their illumination,
And how much inspired and dedicated they are
To the example of those who shed the light.
The men in whom shines the spirit of revelation
Call other men to come to them,
And the other men see how the dead spirit in them
Rises to the call of the awakened spirit.
May the awakened ones ever wake up the sleeping ones,
Bringing forthwith the heaven on this earth.

This frame of flesh has all the innate power;
But who will give the call?
Who will wake in man ecstasies of a wonderful future?
Who will scale the walls of his prejudices?
Who will kindle the spark of his love?
Though provided with independent personalities,
We behave as mass of men,
And we awaken not our sleeping conscience.
We are conditioned by a pattern of thinking,
We move in a course set for us.
We behave not as independent entities,
But herds and followers of so many camps.
We bear not the stamp of our individuality,
But are like so many coins of the same mint.
If only we were prepared
To be our own in face of mass hysteria,
To evolve a method of approach inspired by our

conscience,
And to fully exploit the strength of love.
If we only decided to keep on the side of love;
If we just decided to stand under the sunshine of love,
We could call a halt to this march towards our doom.
But how often our leanings towards love are prevented
By the chain of social customs,
By the retrograde thinking of many a mass of men,
And by our refusal to see the signal of our flaring flame,
Beckoning us, wanting us to be in harmony with everything,
And warning us to keep away from the hatred of anything.
Thus we in the frame of flesh, kept alive by a strange mystery,
Know not whose call to obey—that of overbearing nature of our flesh
Or of silent whisperings of our heart.
For one is powerful to force us to remain on its set track,
Requiring us to fulfil our basic desires and thereafter to grow in flesh,
Raise enough fat, look like a glutton, and have the appearance of an insatiable animal.
The other one, the silent whisperings of our heart,
Wants to bring us in touch with our longings for love—
The call from our constant burning flame,
To give this frame of flesh beauty, lustre and grace,
To bring our frame of flesh in harmony with our flame,
And to illumine our path by the light of that flame.

Thus these frames of flesh,
The mass of women and men,
They all yearn to be in harmony with their flames.
Thus starts our quest, and we, bearing these frames
Do need to listen to the whisperings from within,

And set before ourselves the aim and goal of our journey.
Those who listen inside pass their journey in peace.
Others trying to adjust their frames with outer world cause them intense pain,
Often hurt them, often bring them to a forced end.
The frame of flesh as long as it carries flame
Should be carried with grace and tenderness,
And lightly too,
For does it bear anything else than flame?

There are frames whose flames acquire a brighter light,
Who outlive their mortal frames on the strength of their flames;
Whose good deeds and noble thoughts while in the state of their being,
Fulfil the quest of their restless flames.
Who emit light, love and hope
Beyond the limitations of time,
Beyond the memory of history,
And beyond the annals of any records.
It is such ever-shining flames that bless flames of humbler beings,
That awaken them from their sleep of yore,
That stir them from their lethargic pose,
To enable them to awake to life's realities,
To do their tasks in tune with the eternal flame,
And to follow the path inspired by quest of flame.

In each one of us, in the frame of flesh of all of us,
Flame stands as a beggar, seeking alms from higher and nobler flames.
In remembering them, in being granted a part of their grace
We achieve a blessedness.
And we mortal beings reach an ecstasy,

Lighted by flame, ever in constant quest.

In seeking our quest, we are answering the call of our flame.
Till the flame in us can import light from other flames
We appear again and again in repeated births
Till we can strongly kindle our own flame.
Flames that shine as immortal names
Are ever in tune with other flames,
Giving them the strength to follow them.
Thus frames of flesh move in the world,
Seeking a flame stronger in light than their own flames,
And ever trying to achieve a brighter light for them.
Flame ever goes to a brighter flame and thus we mortal ones
Praise the power and strength of brighter flames.
In remembering them, in seeking their example.
In understanding them,
In listening to their ideas,
In knowing about their experiences,
And in treating them as superior ones,
We are partaking a light once shed by them.
In this way, all weaker and humbler flames
Are ever wanting to be stronger and brighter ones.
Like this all over the world flames are ever seeking a higher meaning of life,
And our quest shall continue till all the flames acquire the same strength and light.
Till then, frames of flesh shall ever move,
Till then, our mortal frames shall pursue their quest,
And we will ever be in an upsurge without a rest,
Till we reach the goal of our journey's end.

## XVI

# Music

From a distant land I hear soft notes of music—
Enthralling, enveloping, and calling me to themselves.
Silently and softly, quietly and gently
I wake up from my slumber as I hear a familiar voice
Calling me, and pointing out the way for me to follow.

As I rise and shake myself of my sleep,
And open the doors of my mind
I see a vision of great beauty and delight.
My mind flutters, and like a bird flies away to the sky.
Traveling alone in its sojourn,
It sees not what is to its left and right,
It is on its way to a vision of rare delight.

Thus my mind is tuned to the notes I have heard.
There is a land from where they come, and to which they are calling me.
Not in this birth, but in distant past when I did not have the present garb.
I had heard them too.
Immortal, known only to the recesses of my heart,
Those notes are being struck again,
They will conquer and overpower my tender heart
And lift it to an ethereal world.

These notes are nearing me, they are louder now.
My spirit stands still and knows how the notes will move.
In what manner they will rise and how they'll fill my life,
How every limb and part will feel the music's thrill,
And how I shall expand to their size.

They have ever been here, there and everywhere.
Only we lack the light, how the notes are tuned.
Only we lack the knowledge, how they are made.
Only we know not their secret hidden place.

Music has a secret tryst with heart's subtler veins.
There are patterns of notes that my heart specially knows,
And when such notes get struck they wake my sleeping heart,
Leading my heart to lose all contacts with the outer world,
Making my mind a slave of this melodious world.

Music, you are an all-pervasive picture of melody, art and rhythm,
A sweet concert of love, hope and emotion;
A rare thing that delights countless millions.
Music, you are a delicate composition of nothingness
To which I have tried to give a shape.
Music, you are like an echo of unfulfilled dreams,
But you gush before me like a dancing stream.
Music, I am held spell-bound by your enchanting thrill
That has entwined me like a lost beloved.

Music, does any one know of your birth
And does any one know from where you call?
Does any one know from where you echo
And does any one know from where you get your power?

Music, my journey will shortly end.
But wherever you come from and wherever you go to,
Your journey will never end, your journey will ever last.
In ever new forms, ever fresh and ever beautiful,
You will inspire and enthrall the spirit of man.

## XVII

# Children come from the dreamland of wonder

Children come from the dreamland of wonder,
Where they lived in the world of their fancies;
Where they ever smiled and were ever gay;
Where they did nothing else except to sleep and play.

It was a land where lived many fairies
Who sang many songs and told many tales.
In the world of their own they knew just nothing;
Their world was full of wonders of which they knew alone.

In the dreamland of wonder there was none to love them.
So they neither faced growth nor ever met decay.
In the dreamland of wonder they knew not what was love.
In search of love the children left their hearth and home.

In the land of this world love was in waiting.
But wonder became a dream when they came to this world.
Though they reached this world, yet forgot about the wonder.
They now always chase the wonder, having forgotten their world.

When they lie in reverie of their past lovely days,
Of the time they had spent in the dreamland of wonder.
They often smile in sleep when they recall the fairy tales
Which they were told while they were in the dreamland

of wonder.

This world is very different from the dreamland of wonder.
In the dreamland of wonder no knowledge was required.
In the world of our own one has to know a great deal,
Despite all the wisdom brought from the dreamland of wonder.

In the dreamland of wonder, nothing ever decayed.
In this world, they knew not they would have to grow up.
For, in this world things grow up and then they get decayed
Which never happened to any one in the dreamland of wonder.

At the birth of children people are so happy.
They little know that children were far more happy
In the dreamland of wonder where there was no barter,
While in this world of reality there is so much of barter.
Here innocence is sacrificed for being crafty.
Here wisdom is mortgaged to acquire a little ignorance.
Here wise have to be foolish for being worldly-wise.
For how can one be worldly without being worldly-wise.

In the dreamland of wonder there was no truth, no falsehood.
There everything was a wonder; here everything is good or bad.
Children when they come here are often perplexed,
For they know not how can truth have a rival in the world.

In the dreamland of wonder there was no poverty.
There every one had so much that no one knew of wealth.
Though all children come begging of someone to love them,

Yet soon they are made different in poverty or in wealth.

In the dreamland of wonder there was neither past nor present,
For no one was ever born nor any one ever died.
Here, in this world there is a past history,
And children have to learn all that happens in the world wide.

In the dreamland of wonder there was no need of knowledge;
All that existed was known to each and every one.
But often in this world one must learn from nothing,
Because all that exists here is not known to every one.

In the dreamland of wonder no one was clever.
So in this world they thought innocence was enough.
But soon they learnt one had to be a little clever.
How otherwise could they exist in so selfish a world?

In the dreamland of wonder no one ever quarrelled.
So they came in this world thinking no one ever quarrelled.
But in the land of this world people so often quarrel.
As children they understand not why should one quarrel.

At the time of their birth they were called by their mothers,
Who wanted them as someone whom they could love.
They were so contented in the dreamland of wonder.
But in this world they have often to cry for their mothers.

As all of us have come from the dreamland of wonder,
We should be those often dreaming in wonder.
While the children do have some link with the dreamland of wonder,
Do the grown-ups ever dream or even at all wonder?

# XVIII
# To the Young Women of India

Oh, you young women of India,
From where have you found your once lost soul.
How have you awakened from your endless dope?
How have you discovered your own proud heart?
How have you decided to change your path?
How do you walk in great esteem?
How strong you walk with an air of your own?
How determined you are with views of your own?
How can you stop if you are part of a stream?

How did they look, your yesterdays?
You are a gift of time to the modern age.
It was a silent sea till it was yesterday,
But today you are a part of a stormy sea.
Your heart cannot contain your old furies,
Servile to men and living on crumbs,
And slaves to their many whimsical ends.

Today you stand as fiery as men were yesterday.
Can any one stop the tide of your hidden fury?
Verily you are the embodiment of great '*Shakti*'.
In your heart burns a fire of great zeal,
To recover the time lost in one quick stride,
To reach the top and even touch the sky.

You are impatient of the weight of the shameful past.
You are possessed of many a glorious dream.
Who has roused you from your slumber to a mighty roar?
Who has given you a new vision you knew not before?

You look not to the left nor to the right.
Please devour not everything that may come in your sight.
Wear not the look of fire and beware of many a slip.
Possess your power, but be not possessed by it.

You are makers of our motherland,
Oh young women, pray be worthy of it.

# XIX

# *Oh woman, you are one half dream and one half true*

Oh woman, you are one half dream and one half true.

In long distant past when no man was born,
When nothing that could live, existed at all,
You were conceived as the cause and purpose of the world—
For fulfilment of man's designs so that he could have a reason to live;
For being his companion so that he could have a purpose to exist,
And for making the world a lovely and beautiful thing.

Then you came alone in a dark night, groping for your path,
Not knowing what else you should do,
And for fulfilment of the cause that the world might live,
Woman, you gave a start to this eternal life.

In this endless chase of discovery of what you are,
The man has spent his entire life.
Your one half lives in this world, the half that the man loves;
The half of which he is the master and lord;
The half which is gay and bright.

It is the other half, the treasure of your longings for eternity

Which holds the key to your heart,
The half which is full of mystery.
It is that half that eludes the spirit of man,
That makes woman the despair of man,
The great puzzle of life.

She may be a beauty of great rarity;
She may be a master-piece of God's designs;
She may be anything and everything,
There is a shadow that follows her in every prize;
The shadow that mystifies the minds of men.

What is that she thinks when she does not talk?
What is that she laughs when she could cry?
What is that she cries when she could laugh?
What is that she hopes when all is lost?
What is that she loves which men cannot?
What is that she sees that others do not?
What is all that she longs for, when she has everything?
In everything something is always missing and lost.
It is the mystery of what is missing that perplexes the minds of men.

Oh woman! you are one half real, the other half appears to be a dream.

No one has ever conquered a woman's heart.
A man could have stormed the fort of a woman's heart.
A man could have scaled the walls of a woman's heart.
But has a man ever conquered a woman's heart.

It is the lot of the man to say, "I admit defeat."
It is for the man to admit and say, "I have lost."
But does a woman ever admit defeat?
Does a woman ever give in as lost?

She stays and the most powerful of men fall before her in defeat.

There is something in the other half that the man knows not.
It is the other half of her mind that gives her power and mystery.
A woman beside you is only one half true;
The other half is a great mystery.

# XX

## Youth

I thought I could be young again.
Ageing is one's life-long problem.
One never knows where youth ends and old age starts.
Youth opens its door only for once;
It remains thereafter shut;
And one spends the rest of one's life in trying to open the door.

As a child the longing is to be young;
As young the excitement is to enjoy.
And then, till one remains alive,
It becomes a ceaseless chase in pursuit of youth.

Till one dies one is seized of this mirage of life,
Never realized, but always enamoured of its enchanting spell;
Always trying to hold the slippery youth
Which is always running away.

Youth, you are the most elusive thing of life.

## XXI

# Why is the present running away without a kiss?

Why is the present running away without a kiss?
Yesterday is lost to the memory of the dead past;
Tomorrow is yet to be born unknown to any one.
Why should the present be running away without a kiss?

Look! man is being born as a gift of the unknown to the immediate present.
See! he is going to wed; he was losing his race against this powerful present.
There, he is dead as a relic of the present to the sad and wailing past.
Thus he is forgotten to lie deep and buried in the unknown past.

I sit a while to stop the present from running away.
I send for the musicians and my friends to celebrate the present.
But everything takes its own time to be able to be present,
While the present is laughingly and mockingly running away.

In the company of my beloved I sit to clasp the present.
To make her a present, of my present, I give her my love.
I had sat when it was night, and then I was awake.
Now the world is awake, while night is gone, where is my present?

The day is hollow, and I have already exhausted the present.
Fatigued and sleepy, I have been befooled by the present.
Where is that present which could not stop and ran away?
Where is that present, and when and why did it run away?

Sometimes I sit in gloom of the time that I have lost,
Brooding over past, in the present, fleeing into past,
Forsaking the present, so dear to me, for the sake of the past;
The mighty tide of the present riding high and defeating me.

There I lie fallen and defeated by the powerful present;
Sad and brooding, and wasting the gift of the priceless present.
Not trying at all to stop the present from running away;
Not knowing at all where is the present slipping away.

Let me wed the dreams of future with the present.
Let me bless and bind the two in eternal bliss.
Let me make the present, the most precious present.
And stop the present from running away without a kiss.

Stop dear present! and take this present, as my present,
Give to the present, my dearest present, the very present.
Love only the present in every moment of the present,
And let not the present run away without a kiss.

Unborn time! be kind to me.
Bless me with the happy present whose every moment I must enjoy.
Immediate present! be gentle to me.
Keep me bound with the silken threads of your tenderness.

## XXII

# Day! you rise as is put round your neck, a garland of the golden rays of the sun

Day! you rise as is put round your neck, a garland of the golden rays of the sun.
To herald that bright and beautiful ceremony children, women and men,
Birds and animals, all move to wake and make noises as like their minds.
Buds open into flowers, dew into pearls and air into fragrant breeze,
And then in all those parts of the world that are so blessed,
Rises day and a great event comes about,
The day comes, lo! the day comes.

Day! you arrive so quietly, so silently and so unobtrusively.
All those who live to see you arrive feel that they are alone alive,
And pray in thankfulness that they have lived for one more day.
Oh day! you arrive like surprize itself personified.

What events are hidden in the womb of unborn time?
What history is concealed in the hours that have to go by?
What heroes have to be born before the day will also be out?

How many of us will have died, before you, day will also die?

Where do you go as the sun sets everyday behind the sky?
Which worlds do you bless when our one you do not light?
How secured do we feel as the fresh day blossoms in the morn?
And then starts the journey of the day that has just been born.

Everyday that is born is heavier than the day left behind.
It carries the burden of the past, its conflicts and crimes.
And as the time passes on, relentless, brutal and unkind,
It resolves disputes, settles claims, and leaves nothing to rescind.

It levels all and everything just by the passage of powerful time.
As the day gathers its force, and as it moves on to its destined end
The peak of full activity is reached in the afternoon;
And then it moves to the sad evening and shiveringly meets its end.

The morning brings freshness, coolness, beauty and softness;
The day introduces vigour, velocity, stride and strength;
The noon leads to activity, haste, hurry and heaviness;
And the evening is full of fatigue, exhaustion, retirement and end.

So many of the days will go by, and so many of them will arrive.

Everyday has its importance, everyday its significance.
Some man was born on some day, some was wedded on some day.
Some was blessed on one day, and some would die on one day.
No one has seen the unborn day, no one has seen the unborn time.
A day that is born has joined the past, and the time that is here has been left behind.

Day! you are the only thing that does not live,
You are the most fleeting thing of life.
No one has lived the unborn day, no one has clenched the unborn time.
In this old chronicle of ephemeral life,
I was born, I lived, and I died;
And these days passed mockingly by.

# XXIII

## Holi

The inhibitions that circumscribe men are today gone.
In tune with the riot of nature the men too are at riot.
Peasants after endless waitings of long wintry nights
Feel the warmth of the rising sun.
Their hearts treasure many hopes, and they look fondly
at the things around.
Their fields are rich with fruits, flowers and crops.
Not long ago they had sown these, and knew not
What would be the outcome as their reward.
And now they see nature in gay abandon—
The crops swinging in full bloom of their youth,
The animals, the dumb millions carrying joy in their
eyes.
The world, sitting like a lovely bride
Is dreaming of her honeymoon with spring.
Everywhere the world is aglow with the warmth of its
youth;
Everywhere there is a fresh fragrance and a new smile.

The men in the workshops, the clerks, the traders, the
wealthy men—
All find nature overflowing with a new expectation.
The body languishes and is filled with a sweet lingering
pain.
The heart is full of many dreams of love,
And eyes see a new colour in every form.

The nature wears a new shape,
Like the dancing girl appareled in lovely hues—
Bearing a twinkle in her eyes, a smile on her lips,

A heave on her bosom, and a swing on her hips,
Who, as in the beginning of a dance, makes a slow beat,
Slowly filling the air with her magic sight.
It is a sight that transcends description.
Everything wears a cloak of hope
As if a long cherished desire is just to be fulfilled.
The time gone by was just a preparation for this day
When men's merriment would know no bounds;
When women's joy would spill over their faces,
And when children would not be bound to any end.

The signal is given by the beat of a heavy drum,
And every one jumps in a dance of joy, raising clouds of many colours.
Pink, red, yellow, blue, green all are smeared on faces,
And the men wear a multicoloured look, like nature
Which is limitless in colour, joy and form.
On the '*Holi*' day there is no beginning no end.
There is only one cry heard all over the land—'*Holi hai*', '*Holi hai*.'

# XXIV

# *So bashful became my boyhood eight years past*

So bashful became my boyhood eight years past
That it slipped away and never took my leave.
Had I ever known that I was in life's unknown bliss,
Where there was neither love nor pain;
Where there was neither remorse nor gain,
I would have for ever clung to its feet.
But life lacked test at the anvil of time that only experience taught,
And one strange morning I was in a mysterious garb.

I felt I had a self that in silent whispers spoke;
I had a self that broke through limbs which ached;
Eyes lowered themselves when silent steps they heard;
Heart leapt out when an unknown face it saw;
And a mystery woke in me, so subtle its meaning was.
That day I felt I never should have been born,
So desperate waiting was.
The nights wove in themselves hopes that shadows gave;
The shadows broke my heart when suddenly they would pass.
I found there was an image that I could catch
But it ran far and far.
I felt a pain rise in me and break my heart,
Leaving me like a soul lost in a mysterious garb.

I thought of my boyhood which was wedded to mystery;
I thought of my boyhood protected by purity;

I thought of my boyhood shielded by innocence;
I thought of my boyhood spent in full abandon.
And then I stood face to face with life's strange subtleties;
And then I knew not what was my goal and aim of life;
I knew not how could I cover my shame, and cry and cry.

My boyhood had left me sad and alone, and
I had lost as if a treasured belonging.
I thereafter entered a new phase of life.
I thereafter climbed the footsteps of life.
I was knocked about wherever I went,
And joined myriads and myriads of men.

## XXV

*When I grew to be eighteen, you suddenly came into my life to coincide with the birth of my love*

When I grew to be eighteen, you suddenly came in my life to coincide with the birth of my love.
I had only known that life was full of fun and play, to be happy and gay.
Love was known to me like the outer appearance of an attractive fruit;
Not knowing its inner form, its taste, and what lay inside the fruit.

I was like a flower recently born, and grown only into a bud,
Whose petals were not yet open as it did not have any warmth.
And you secretly arrived to open the bud of my youth by your warmth.
What was that that excited you that you chose me as your bud?
Why did you cling to me and said, "I must open you by my love."
Of course, you did succeed in seeing the colour of my petals;
You did succeed in opening the petals of my love.
But you also opened the gate of new emotions in flood.
I did admire you, how lovely you looked in your black and beautiful eyes.

With the silken touch of your caresses you did try to awaken my sleeping life.
Your body was overflowing to the brim with the foam of your youth.
Every limb you moved, and every gesture you made left me restless all the more.
Often your words left many things unsaid what your silence later on explained.
When you smiled I felt the world was smiling with you.
When I found you frown with fury and hate, I felt the world had a bad taste.
You appeared to me to have been born like the morning of life,
Where noon had yet to come and evening was far away.
You made me conscious of my life and you gave a glimpse of what lay in your heart—
Its mysteries, its hopes, its agonies and its smart.
Once I did know that a man did need a woman, and that I was born for you.
You awoke in me hopes for tomorrow, overfilling me with dreams for you.
I was a free bird till yesterday, but I was imprisoned by you.
I could have moved alone, innocent as I was, but you wrapped me with the love worn by you.
I had thought I could have stood and fought the menace of your tenderness,
But you overwhelmed me by laying open before me your restlessness.
I had thought I could have run away from the closed atmosphere of your love,
But you took me out in the open air and let me go with a gentle touch.
I did want to run away from you, I did think of deserting you,

But you were so fully frank that you bound my heart to your love.
I did want to tell you how I loved you much.
I did come near that stage, I did come to the state of announcing my love.
But at the zero hour I found you in company of those I could not love.
Then I was jealous of those, I thought, who stole your love.
You made me feel that others had a special place, whom you loved,
And you made me feel I was not after all needed so much.
Still, sometimes you brought the cup of your love near my lips;
But you took it away no sooner you thought than it would be sipped.
My love! do you know how in this trick you badly failed.
Though by your clever ways you did arouse my anguish and hate,
Yet it made me wiser, it made me understand a women's subtle ways.

But now, when I think in retrospect, I imagine you wanted me to prize you as the only one.
I knew not then, though I know it now, that you wanted to be my only one.
But then you wanted to test my innocence by your clever and polished ways,
You wanted to test my purity through your cunning ways.
The petals of my love did open then at least for once;
The dew of my hopes did settle there at least for once;
The butterfly did sting me with the poision of love though for once;
Yet that one chance was lost by you to your superior and clever ways.

Not all the petals of my love opened, and not all of them ever came into full bloom.
Some petals were found withering away, and some were found in part of their gloom.
The bud of my love did open again but not without pain.
Though there were many others who did try to console me, yet it was all in vain.

Oh my love, why did you forsake me when you could have been mine?
Whose heart had come so near me, my love, except thine?
Why did you become only a shadow when you were really with me?
When I wanted to be yours, and only yours, why you just forgot me?
Was there any one who knew the smell of your breath except me?
Was there any one who knew the taste of your lips except me?
Was there any one who knew the beat of your lonely heart except me?
Was there any one who could have wiped the tears from your eyes except me?
Was there any one who could have helped you to get into a stride except me?

Why did you invite me so often if you wanted to despise me?
Why did you call me back again if only to surprise me?
Why did you not take me at what I was then worth?
Why did you think that I had a hidden self besides myself?
Why did you think that I would swear my love even though you made me feel sad?
Why did you not think that I, for one, wanted to be

simple and straight?
How can I ever forget the opening in my heart you have made?
How can I ever heal the wound bleeding that is still agape?
How can I ever overcome your longings that still visit me in my dreams?
In anguish you do visit my heart when often I helpless seem.
In misery I come to you for sympathy whenever I find not any one else.
In separation you try to console me that I am not without someone else.
But why did you leave me, when together we would have been one?
Why did you play false with me when we could have for ever been one?

## XXVI

# Dream

My mind is lost in the stream since I had a dream of you.
Your glistening eyes call me in, and drown me deep.
I struggle to come out, and find you not.
Your image comes and vanishes in one stream of dream, where are you?

In the lullaby of my lovely dream you beside were me.
Your hands crossed my eyes, and I thought
It was my friend who had come beside the stream.
I caught hold of them, and gently asked,
"Why do you play hide and seek with me?"
Could I have ever said that to you
If I ever knew that it was you?

My mind is lost in the stream since I had a dream of you.
My heart stands imprisoned in your loving heart;
My smile sealed in your whispering lips;
My steps caught in the way of your house beside the stream.

My body pines in love, drunk deep in the wine of your youth.
I am in your memory caged, when will you come my love?

My dream will come true, when again I see you beside the stream.
My mind is lost in the stream of dream since I had a look of you.

# XXVII

# *So you have come*

So you have come.
My heart had often wandered in your search,
But the world was wide and you had left no trace of your whereabouts,
And I had often wondered if you would ever return.

Once our eyes had chance met in an unwritten agreement of our hearts.
Since then I had carried the picture of your sweet face secretly treasured in my heart.
Only when I was alone did I open the treasure box to have a silent glance
So that the world would never learn of our secret love.

Now that you have come why do you talk to me only through your glances.
Though I follow what you say, yet why don't you speak,
And why don't you say what is hidden in your heart.

Why do you scold me like this, and not even utter a single word?
No, not even once did I ever betray the secret of our love;
No, not even for a second did I ever think of anything else but you;
And still you don't believe me and my sacred love.

When there were the days of the full-moon and I would lie to sleep on the terrace of my little house,
I had often asked the moon if she knew the way to your distant house,

Or if she had any clue of your unknown sojourns.
Though no one could have thought of me sane, yet I knew,
And even the moon had stood silent,
And told me that wherever you were, you would one day return.

When it used to be cold and long wintry nights,
And when the winds would shriek through the creaks of our windows, I had often heard you calling me;
And then the nights were so cold that even dogs would not dare to bark;
And I used to think those shrieks were yours and I would run out of my house,
And walk aimlessly in the streets in those dark and dreadful nights.
Though I heard everywhere your frightening shrieks, yet where were you?

Why should tears come in your eyes, oh you still don't believe me
Because you think that no man will refuse an invitation to a woman's heart,
So fickle and false he is supposed to be in love.
And that is why you think that I just pretend to be in love;
And thus you are in doubt, and you want to be sure of my heart.

Oh! Why do you heave such deep sighs of forsaken love?
Let me assure you I never meant to hurt you at all.
I know in the secret chambers of your bosom
You must be treasuring the longings of your meetings with me.
Is that what is forcing your heart to leap at me?
Pray, think not that you alone suffered for me.

Why don't you come near me even though I have often beckoned you?
How can the walls of separation disappear unless we be one?
How can I drown your sorrows of the dark nights of separation unless we be one?

Please do not laugh like this.
It makes me feel that you have not taken my love seriously.
Why is your joy bursting through all your limbs,
And why can't you contain your smile on your glowing face?
What is that you have robbed me of that you feel so wealthy in possessing?
Now you feel confident like the merchant with no competitor of the wares to sell.
So you are convinced that you have vanquished me well.
And no one can ever snatch me away from you and from the prison of your heart,
And you can do to me what commands your proud and smiling heart.

## XXVIII

# When you are away

When you are away,
Everything I love and like is lost.
Hope is lost, zest is lost, and fun is lost
When you are away.

Nights are as calm as ever before;
Nights are as stormy as ever before.
When nights were calm you told me so.
You told me so and made me calm.
Nights were often stormy I could see them so;
You came near me and would not let me go.

The sun rises as well as ever before;
Days are as warm as ever before;
Evenings are as hopeful as ever before;
But you are away.

Everyday of your stay leaving me away
Is like a lifetime spent.
Every expression of your face, every move you made
Is now what I cannot scan.

What led you away, what stood in your way, I cannot say.
You said, "I would go away." And away you went.

# XXIX

# My fair friend, the sight of you is a wonderful thing

My fair friend, the sight of you is a wonderful thing.
In the prime of your youth, fresh like a flower,
In the glory of your beauty, ripened like an invitation,
Your hue holds a lovely smile, and your passion for life
Makes me feel that life is a worthy thing.
Why is it that I shower my love and thoughts on you?
In the weary world, torn with care and strife,
You are an island in the stormy sea
Where I can anchor my heart to rest a while,
And think that life is not a useless thing.
I say, look towards me for a while.
Do not forsake the smile that keeps you fresh.
Like me many a one draws his strength from your sight,
For your sight which is such a wonderful thing.

## XXX

# When I would cease to see the light of the day

When I would cease to see the light of the day;
When the sun, moon and stars would no longer rise for me;
When I would move not as I did everyday,
I would have passed on to the realm of eternity.
Today I move about, master of my own life;
Sometimes in doubts, and sometimes free of doubts.
But of tomorrow I know not whether it will rise,
And how can I be sure of my future because of my doubts.
Though every one lives in constant fear of death,
Yet no one thinks ever of the time of one's end.
One is in love with one's friends, but not with one's death,
Death, which is the best and the only permanent friend.
Thus I sit and brood in the shadow of my life,
Being cast by the powerful and omnipotent death.

# XXXI

# When I look upon the lot of the people around me

When I look upon the lot of the people around me,
I think of the purpose with which they may be seized.
Then I grieve over the aimlessness with which they are seized,
And I know not what goads them in their activities.
Driven by an unknown force, they move from place to place;
Met by many accidents, they give up not their old ways.
Thus women and men move about in sheer aimlessness,
And in bearing sad and strange blank-facedness.
On looking upon such lot of people around me
I am filled with frustration and great dejection;
I am seized by a feeling of extreme exasperation.
Then I feel so ill at ease and so void of peace.
Then I think of art that may give men some purpose;
And I wonder and wonder, why men do not have any purpose.

## XXXII

# When in review of the present times

When in review of the present times,
I think of the events that are all round spread;
Then I think of the people who make their lives upset,
And who undertake tasks without application of mind.
Then I have many a tear to shed in regret
How logic and reason have from our noble land fled.
I see men blinded by ignorance, and misled by superstition
Even in the present advanced scientific times.
Thus many a life has suffered not in crime
But in being seized by stupid and silly convictions.
Thus the mind frustrates and one wastes one's breath
In discussions not based on reason or rhyme.
Such are the trends with which we are faced,
And know not how to reconcile present with the future times.

## XXXIII

# Drowned in the humdrum of busy life

Drowned in the humdrum of busy life;
Not finding time to think, unable to get a respite;
I feel that my real self has gone on a holiday,
And a mechanical device in me operates.
Thus the world thinks I am alive,
Sees me walk and move about in life,
Imagines that that is really I in bone and flesh.
But where am I? I often ask myself.
Not in my office, not in my house,
For I hear no inner voice, I harbour no doubts.
No misgivings arise, no thoughts are at play.
I am as if gone to a different place,
Which point, which place, I cannot locate,
Because I am reduced to such a blank state.

## XXXIV

# When I return from many a distant sojourn

When on return from many a distant sojourn,
I question myself whether I am the one who has returned.
For on return to the same place or town
One finds it different from what one left behind.
So one knows not what is true,
The one who has returned, or the place that looks new.
Surrounded by a halo of great surprise,
One knows not what is right.
Whether the place one has come back is real
Or the place from which one has come is a dream.
Whether the state of being awake is real
Or the state of being in a dream,
Whether death is what is real,
And life but all a dream.

## XXXV

# As I move along the years of my advancing age

As I move along the years of my advancing age,
I think often of those who are younger than I.
I think of the time I had spent when I was young,
And of the time spent by those who are younger than I.
My mind becomes heavy with the burdens of my past,
And how everyday I am growing old, look alas.
The twinkle of my dreams, the music of my songs
Are now seized by those who have just become young.
My yesterdays mock at me through the youth of the young.
They tell me of the fleeting nature of the time I had spent.
Ah, today I feel having lost so much of my life,
Having entered the threshold of the noon of my life.
Now tears come in my eyes that I too am growing old,
Even I am not being spared the tragedy of being old.

## XXXVI

# The journey to Taj is like a pilgrimage

The journey to Taj is like a pilgrimage.
In far distant lands,
In the minds of men and women all over the world,
Wherever its name has been heard,
It has cast a magic spell.
Every one who has ever heard
About the immortal love of a man for his wife;
For him Taj has worked like a call from a distant land,
To India—the beautiful and enchanting land,
Where men and women have come on a pilgrimage
To see this image of undying love.

The love, the passion, the immortal bond
Is cast in every stone, in every dome.
At every step a cry is heard, of love, of everlasting love,
Of the love of Mumtaz Mahal and Shah Jahan[1].
For three decades and five, he lived alone with eyes glued
To this enchanting spell.
On this monument millions of men spent their lives
To entomb one dead.
Shah Jahan, you truly loved your wife,
And true to her you also lie
Beside her dead.

Mighty in its majesty, glorious in its beauty, shining in its

---

1  Shah Jahan was the Emperor of India during 1627 and 1658. Mumtaz Mahal was his wife.

splendour,
This dreamland on earth is a sacred place.
Those who prize love over life find it a dedicated place.
It is a pilgrimage whenever love is in doubt;
Whenever any one feels the need to open a new page
He must come to this haloed place and renew his faith.

Taj has a honeymoon with every night.
Taj is celestial on a full-moon night.
Born of a fairy tale, Taj lands on your mind like a dream come true;

Yet too beautiful to be true.
Freshly bathed and dressed in exquisite white,
Every time Taj is a lovely sight.

Its music can be heard:
The endless eternal notes of love,
Coming slowly, coming from a distant land,
Till one feels this is an ethereal world and a page from a dream,
When the world would be at a standstill and there would be no haste.
The journey to Taj is like a pilgrimage.

Those who see Taj must know that it is a tender bond,
Tenderly it stands just touching the heart of every one.
It calls every one to itself embodying the hope of every one,
That he too would be blessed by the same eternal love,
As of Mumtaz Mahal and Shah Jahan.
Every one visits Taj to renew his faith.

The journey to Taj is thrilling as a pilgrimage.

## XXXVII

# It is memory that is everything

It is memory that is everything.
It is image that is the real thing.
Long after the life is spent;
Long after the time is past;
Long after the present sinks;
Long after the dreams depart;
Memory alone lingers like a magic spell.

From the wakeful memories of sweet childhood,
From the fast growth of throbbing womanhood,
From the sweet stealings of ripening manhood,
What remains, are memories that give life the real sap,
That sustain it and carry it on to the end of life.

Has any one ever conquered time?
Has any one ever held even a second in his powerful hand?
It passes on selfishly, relentlessly.
Never merciful, never mindful of those who do not partake in life.

Those who love and those who make the best of life,
As also those who cry, hate and blame all and everything,
Are all carried along, along the surge of a mighty tide.
Some sustained and fed with memories of life,
Well-spent and sweetly-spent,
Make journey a great delight.
Others corroded and dying of hate fall in the journey's end
Without a memory or a sigh.

It is memory that is everything,
That must not die;
That must be cherished along like a treasured thing
Till the end of life.

## XXXVIII

# Flying in an Aeroplane

Look bird, I too can fly.
Like you, I too can move across the sky.
I too can feel the thump of my heart,
When to swing low I come near the earth.

I also can survey the vast regions in one sight.
I also can look upon the world with great pride.
I have now become a part of your great herd,
That comes from one world and flies to another world.

But bird, you are free when you fly.
You are master of everything when you fly.
All the world is yours;
All the land, trees, lakes and rivers belong to you;
The tall mountains, and the remote seas
Are all within your reach.
Everything that you can see belongs to you.
You can land anywhere you choose.
You can perch anywhere you swoop.
But I am bound to many ways.
When I fly, I fly bound in a cage.
I cannot call, the wings even as mine
While you fly without any confine.

## XXXIX

# Today, I write in memory of my old and sweet past

Today, I write in memory of my old and sweet past;
About the days of my boyhood, and about the youth of my past.
About such time and such past when every second treasured a secret dream;
About such days and such periods when I was ever lost in my dreams:
When every moment was a rare delight and a great ecstasy;
When life appeared to have no beginning and no tragedy;
When every passing phase appeared greatly exciting,
And when in the dark corners of future were concealed strange secrets of a hidden thing:
When the present danced like an uninhibited happiness,
And when every event was clothed in a hush-hush business:
When every unimportant thing looked like a great adventure,
And a small development, a happening of far-reaching consequence:
When past appeared like a lingering event from a fairy tale,
And future like a master magician's show:
When mind was unable to comprehend the dividing line between work and play;
When love was not shy of any limitations on its free play;
When friendships were not circumscribed by any wordly considerations;

When every new acquaintance appeared like a fast friend of many lives,
And enmities looked like temporary tides of stormy sea:
When simple knowledge appeared like gems of great discovery,
And any small errand was considered to be a privilege of great responsibility;
Of that my boyhood past, I have many a tender memory.
And of that time when my boyhood slipped into my youth,
Of that period too I carry many silken memories.
Of that time, I cannot write
Without a few tears in my eyes.
For what is left now, are only memories
Of my youth that is already gone.

Youth, when you were awakened from the ageless slumber of old past
You opened your eyes in great surprise as if blessed with a new sight,
And you read a new meaning in everything of life.
Youth, for you, the present appeared wearing a veil of great mystery,
And future was like a mighty effort to unveil that mystery.
For you, love was like a discovery of great significance
Which made many penetrations as it entered deeper into heart;
And which often imparted sweet pain and was as if one's major part.
I think of those days of my youth when experience taught what jealousy was;
When misgivings of rivalry rose slowly in my heart;
When knowledge became the sharp axe with which to cut the jungle of one's ignorance;

When fire burnt in one's heart in defence of one's ideals;
When patriotism radiated like the glowing morning sun;
When motherland appeared like a sacred pledge
Of one's honour for country's defence;
When the task of living appeared to be an easy accomplishment
Like any game in which one was trained;
And when obstacles appeared like goals to be scored
By the co-operation of one and all.
Today I sing the songs of that lovely and exciting past
That was once my youth to me.
And now I am growing old,
Youth having been my last stop.

I sit today grieving over the loss of my youth,
And about the uncertain and anxious present.
There is nothing mysterious about this naked present
Except the seriousness of its realities.
There is nothing beautiful about the blind future
Except the qualification of its uncertainties.
Love is no longer the garland to be woven
With the flowers of one's cherished hopes.
Friendships are no longer the sweet kinships
Binding one in perpetual rope.
Ideals are no longer the sacred pledges,
Of deep dedication for sacrifice.
Life is rather a compromise of convenience with many a silly lie.

The unspent life is now a haunting fear
Of how long will one live and how soon will one die.
So I write in a wistful mood about the memory of my own past life.
I know not what will happen to one any moment,
Such is the burden of the present phase of life.

## XL

# My Dearest Friend!

Many many years past we were like two buds on the same branch.
As you blossomed into a smile, death plucked you apart,
Thus leaving me alone to weep for you.
How little you know of my longings for you;
How near you are my heart when I look at you;
Oh! your face is carved on my weeping heart.

When I gaze at your ever youthful face,
Not looking haggard by the hazards of merciless time,
I think of the wonderful time we had together spent
When we were young.

You are as youthful as shows your deceitful face;
You cheated time and quietly went away.
You were able to overcome your own little age,
Leaving this picture of yours when you were young.

I am lost in the sweet reveries of our youthful days,
And I find you are still young while I am ageing away.
I feel shocked at the growing disparity in our mutual age
Which was the same when we were together young.

# XLI

# *Today, I am bearing a burden of great sorrow*

Today, I am bearing a burden of great sorrow.
I have lost today a dear and beloved one.
Who will come and ask me why I am so sad?
Who will come beside me and join me to be as sad?
And who is there to talk to me through silence sad?

How will I console myself?
Will there be no one to ask me, "Why are you so sad?"
How would I shed my gloom unless others wear a part of it?
How would the gloom wear out unless it is shared by others as well?
Gloom has entered my every part, making me so full of it.
No one knows how much I am bearing it in my head.

I feel like a solitary soul, lost in the doldrum of confusion,
Like a ship rocking wildly on the high tide of tragedy.
Having lost the way of my voyage to the goal of my end,
Disillusioned, thoroughly shaken, and without any aim;
With tears filling me to the brim, thoughts beaten to a solitary track.
Is there any one who will ask me, "Why are you so sad?"

Never has been present so heavy as it seems today;
Never has it moved so slowly as it does today;
And never have been seconds of such heavy gait,
But today the sun has stuck up in the sky, silence in the

air, and moments in my watch;
And I sit like a statue; the world having come to a dead stop.
People talk in whispers, death is mourned by every one,
And I sit unable to comprehend
What has happened to my beloved one.

## XLII

# Death has struck another untimely blow

Death has struck another untimely blow.
Who knew it would arrive from a corner street;
Who knew it would come stealthily and secretly.
A moment gone by I was in my dreamland of fancies,
Musing over life's smooth and even course,
And now I am struck by another untimely blow.

Stupefied and shocked beyond recovery,
I little knew death could be so strong;
And give such a severe blow to leave me blind
Of distance time, and comprehension of my mind.

I now stand alone, bereft of still another friend.
One by one they pick up their satchels and march away
Like school boys always in a hurry to reach their ground of play.
I have been left alone to cry in memory of my departed friends
Who never return from their ground of play,
Though I always wait for their return.

## XLIII

# When I think of the slender thread that holds my heart

When I think of the slender thread that holds my heart,
The little beat that keeps me alive and makes present a fact of life,
I am grieved to think of the morrow that would come to pass
When I am gone and my little heart would cease to give its beat.

How vast looks the world, how big the work of man;
How small is the heart that gives prop to his ambitious plans.
Held by a slender thread, alive by a silent beat,
Heart, you are a wondrous mystery.

Men are held in awe and men are held apart;
Men aspire and have schemes to reach the stars.
Men hate, men love, and men also weep;
All the handiwork of heart, you cute little thing.

Heart, at the end of life you cease to be, and all is an unknown mystery,
Where nothing exists, no wings flutter, and no souls ever meet.

# XLIV

## Sleep

Oh darling sleep, lovely and lulling sleep,
I am a victim of your hypnotic spell.
Sleep, I know not if I was born for you, or
You were born for me,
But I live because I sleep under your caring self.

Sleep, I often wonder if I should question you, who you are.
Sleep, will you answer me? as I am aware not
When and how you steal and hoodwink me.
And little I know where I go, when myself I cease to be.

Sleep, you were born with man,
The only thing that is eternal with man;
The only thing that is never realized;
And yet the only thing that always satisfies.

Sleep, you are the only constant friend;
The only permanent companion that outlives relatives and friends;
The only permanent cure that heals all wounds and vents,
And the only permanent thing that survives one's final end.

And yet I know not what is sleep?
I do not live with it, and know not its qualities.
Yet when it comes it lifts one to a world of fantasies
That one sheds tears on being aware of world's realities.
Sleep separates man from man, woman from woman,
Every one from every one.

It comes individually to every one,
And every one must be himself asleep to sleep.

A task that cannot be entrusted to any one,
For, sleep must itself sleep.

Sleep is like a silent lullaby for transcendence to the world of the unknown.
Sleep is like a daily interval in life's endless and ever-changing scenes.
Sleep is like a short break from life's tragic and pleasant realities.
Sleep is like a silken thread that binds us with our fantasies.

Sleep is like a sharp descent in the world of strange oblivion.
Sleep is the only unifying force in the world's many divisions.
Sleep is the only curtain drawn against bitter and silly fights.
Sleep is the only cause for living and the sweetest chapter of one's life.

Sleep is the only gift of nature that is fully communistic in its designs.
Sleep is the only impartial god that visits everyday every kind.
Sleep is the only efficacious drug, when everything fails, that works.
Sleep is like a small edition of the final end, something that resembles death.
Sleep is one great and wonderful boon for which a man lives and for which he spends.
Sleep is the only priceless treasure which a man possesses but cannot lend.
Sleep is the only great reality that a man must face even when he dies.
For he goes to sleep, as he does everyday,

And as he gets up not, he is known to have died.

How much does any one know where does one go when one goes to sleep?
And yet it is really very little known that a man asleep goes to another world's realm.
While the real men may be living in the unknown world whose counterparts may be in our world asleep,
And our real men may be those ones whose counterparts are in the other world asleep.
And thus the universe may be full of such planets
Where sleep would be the common habit.
And all the planets may be exchanging emissaries
Who may be waking and putting men to sleep in different planets.
And who knows angels may be no one else but emissaries putting men to sleep.
And who could be a more welcome angel than sound and refreshing sleep.

Many people think that to sleep is like to spend one's life in one long dream,
While many others think that to wake is like to spend one's life in an endless dream.
Whatever be it, sleep is one great unsolved mystery,
And no one knows what is the true reality:
The state of being awake or the state of being asleep;
Whether sleep is the only thing real, and living but all a dream.

Of course, the question that remains unsolved is,
Whether one is born to be awake or born to be asleep,
And also no one yet finally knows,
Whether those asleep are the ones who are ever awake,
And those awake are the ones who ever sleep.

# XLV

# We met at the border line

I had a Muslim friend, a very dear Muslim friend,
Whom friends like me had driven away beyond the border line.
He went and settled in another town after crossing the border line.
We both crossed the border line that was of no God's design;
An airy line which was a creation of revengeful minds;
A line that religious enmity had made;
A line that no man could have ever striven to create.
Since then has this line stood stronger than any mighty arms could have ever made.
Men appeared to have then resolved in their hearts that no one with a different faith
Would thereafter live with them;
No matter if they were friends;
No matter how strong were the bonds that held them as one;
All must separate and live beyond the border line.

My friend was very dear and extremely kind to me.
He had in past sent me many gifts and held me in high esteem.
He had asked me often, "What else do you want?"
I had with a twinkle in my eye replied, "It is you that I want."
Such exchanges used to move us to tears and embrace.
Then that line divided us though heart broke to kiss and embrace
My sweet and dear friend who was once so generous and

kind to me.

So much of innocent blood had been spilled in hate.
The hands were red, the land was red, and the eyes were red.
Anger and thirst of blood possessed men, and they said, "We will each other finish away".
The minds of men were overflowing with thoughts of vice and hate;
And they all said, "We will fight, we will fight in the bitterest way.
"We will count, we will count the heads of those who are dead.
"And till we have avenged the number on our side dead, we will not rest."

That many old friends would fight—these thoughts would torture me.
I said, "I must meet my friend. He loves me much, and may be we might die.
"I may be killed by one of his friends and he be killed by one of mine."
I knew the end was not very far, so firmly I resolved
That with immediate dispatch I must meet my friend at the border line.

I had a message sent, "Come my dear friend,
"Not beyond the border line that our thoughts had built .
"We will not cross that line, but we will stand at that line,
"And may be for the last time meet".

We met at the appointed time at the border line.
I said, "You do not look like my friend."
He said, "You do not look like mine."
"What has made us strange, "he said.

I replied, "The border line."
"There is no line that can divide us," we said,
"This is the zero line."
We stood at the zero line and said, "Nobody can instigate.
"We may have different faiths but no one could make us fight.
"So let us sit down and sing a common song." We sang,
"There was a time we had each other greatly loved,
"And then this mental line separated us.
"And now in doubt of our sacred love we meet.
"A Hindu and a Muslim meet at the border line."
We danced and embraced, and those who saw us love in the sea of hate, said,
"The two have gone mad at the border line."

We asked each other of the news since we had last met.
My friend cried and said, "It is sad but my brother is dead.
"His wife, I told her not, I was coming to the border line.
"For, she could have thought I was going to fetch her darling heart.
"She still hopes he will return, and that is what breaks my heart."

I said, "My brother lives, but his wife is held by men of your faith
"At a place hundreds of miles north of the border line.
"She would be crying day and night in separation of her husband and child.
"My brother says he would die than submit to this cruel fate—
"He cries and cries 'My queen, my fair queen has gone away.'"

We talked of our friends who had died.
We talked of the love we had lost.
We talked of the world and said, "Mad has gone the world."
We cried, and tears would not stop.

Over the zero line we met, in each other's lap we lay.
Oh! How two friends had met at the border line.
We kissed and loved, we danced and embraced.
We cried and laughed, we had after all met;
Two friends had after all met at the border line.

# XLVI

# India 1958 Exhibition

Mighty tide of India's destiny, what do I see?
Discovery of India's secret strength.
Replica of India's resurgent soul.
Beauty and greatness of what India is.
Plan and model of what India would be.
Majestic march of a growing lion.
The fond hope of India's many good friends.
The great dream of many a true patriot.
The solid achievement of a proud nation.
The proud glance of a mother at her son's achievements.
Banner of India's strong determination.
Vision of India's wisdom and depth of her knowledge.
Consummation of India's cosmopolitan culture.
Meeting place of many civilizations of the world.
Panorama of what India is.
A bird's-eye view of India, that is *Bharat*.
The picture of a nation shedding its lethargy.
Example of a nation discovering its soul.
Realization of a fond dream.
Fulfillment of a long cherished desire.
The pocket edition of India's great history.
A place of sacred pilgrimage,
The distance covered by our motherland in just one decade.
Merging of science with spirit.
A feat of engineering, industry and perseverance.
Hope and dream of a proud nation.
Plaything of a growing child.
The triumph of peace and democracy.
The present, past and future of India.
A peep into India yet to be.

# XLVII

## My own Punjab

Today, I write of my own Punjab.
Ah, what a land, oh, what a sight.
The land where the heart meets its own delight.
The place where the eyes meet their feast of sights.
Blessed by its lovely past,
Happy in its wonderful present,
Living in just gay abandon,
Greatly hopeful of its bright future,
That land and that place is my own Punjab.

Where fields are ever ripe with many new crops;
Where the land is made fertile by the men of Doab.
The rivers and canals musically irrigate the entire Punjab.
The place where peasants love their land is my own Punjab.

Now Punjab is our nation's one big workshop.
The people love to work hard and they have new ideas;
Full of activity, with artisans engaged in mighty tasks,
To make our dear Punjab the great beloved of India.

Who is there so happy and gay, and who lives in abandon of all the times?
The peasant and worker of the Punjab is in tune with all the times.
He thinks not of the unborn day, he worries not about the spent-up time.
He marches on celebrating the present as the biggest event of all the times.

The peasant lives in tune with the tempo of life.
The worker believes in working with all his might.
The common man is sure of the destiny of his fond Punjab.
The entire state is busy in building a new Punjab.
It is no longer the land of those rivers that gave it its name.
It is no longer the place so big which gave it its fame.
But even when the land was in slavery, the people were free.
Even though the Punjab is now divided, the people live in ease.

You may break this or merge this, its spirit has its own.
It has many of its qualities which are all over known.
Here people live for the sake of living;
Here people love for the sake of loving.

They are active and efficient, they are sturdy and happy.
They work and they preserve, they work and they deserve.
They know this place is theirs, they know this land is theirs.
They are not afraid of any one, they are not concerned in any one.

When it is time to love, they love full well;
When it is time to fight, they fight full well;
When it is time to hit, they hit one hard;
When it is time to eat, they devour all.

Of course, they get along quite practically.
They have sturdy commonsense politically.
They are full of tremendous energy.
They are full of boundless industry.

They are proud of their own grand lands.
They work hard with their own strong hands.
Virile, jolly and sturdy is their race,
And they show a great pride in their honest face.
Where milk is consumed in plenty, and which is the nation's granary;
Where fruit is eaten abundantly, and where food is shared fraternally;
Where living is for good eating, and eating is for happy living;
And where life is to be spent in gaiety without worrying for anything.

Where people play many outdoor games;
Where people are happy without any shame;
Where those in hate are in love today;
Where those in love might even hate today.
Though they live with all and they quarrel with all,
Yet they can live together as if they had never quarrelled.

When they sing it is for the love of the forlorn;
When they dance it is in complete abandon.
When they talk it is even for the deaf to hear it;
When they argue it is for the world to hear it.

They plan as if it is for military operations.
They make preparations as if for mighty celebrations.
They take big decisions as if they are the leaders of the nation.
They are bursting with joy when it is time for big ovation.

Who is there to stop them when it is time for work?
Who is there to restrain them when they are all in upsurge?
Who is there to bind them when they decide to be free?

Who is there to resist them when they are full of glee?

Meet their womenfolk, second to none in love:
Whose brothers are so boundless in sacrifice and love;
Whose husbands are bound so strongly in tender threads of love;
Nothing is greater for them than their love for their own child,
It is always first.
Who is there to outbeat them
For their zest and for their love.

They love all what is theirs,
They clasp what comes in their way.
Pioneers in many new fashions,
They live in a louder way.

They love good dress, they have good form,
And they love colours bright and gay.
Who is there to stop them
When they are all out to sway?

In the many corners of the motherland,
Howsoever you may be away from your own land,
There you will find many ones from my own band,
Where is required an enterprising and a brave hand.

They take to agriculture as if it were the only culture.
And though they often thunder, so many times they also blunder.

Punjab is the land famous for its Nangal and *Bhakra*.
Punjab is the land where they play *Kikli* and *Bhangra*.
Punjab is the land well known for its many canals.
Punjab is the province beloved of one and all.

## XLVIII

# Ganga

You are purer than pure water;
Purer than the purest of diamonds,
Majestic, self-confident, flowing with an innocent conscience,
Crystal-clear, and exquisite in your charm and beauty,
Peaceful, calm and lovely in your matchless serenity.
Ganga, you flow, endless in your love,
Limitless in your benediction,
Boundless in your gentleness,
Like eternal mother.

You were churned from the mass of mountains
As a gift of gods to the inhabitants of *Bharat*.
Ganga, you were born with the world
To make *Bharat* the coveted prize of the world.
There are no annals in the land, no chronicle of the past,
No period in its history, no time that ever passed,
When Ganga, you did not flow.
Is there any man, any sage, any king or any poet
Who did not find you enthralling in your flow?
Ganga, you have been perpetual and eternal in your constant flow.

Ganga, you are ageless as the time, immortal as the universe.
Who would not be lost in the reverie of your deep and silent song?
Who would not be lost in the enchanting beauty of your environs?
Who would not be lost to the magic spell of your

wonderful waves?
And in being absorbed in placid mood of your silent banks.

Flowing in the heart of the land, Ganga, you are like the treasure house of our conscience.
Though shallow as a river, the massive mountains of our sins have been drowned in you;
The darkest of our crimes have been washed by you,
And aimless souls have found a purposeful refuge in you.
Everyday you become purer by the ablution of the unholy of the world.
Mother Ganga, you are verily purity incarnate;
Such is your strength that people hold you in their absolute faith.

Ganga, you inspired our sages to catch a glimpse of the heaven on earth;
To let the unbeliever see the work of the unseen hand;
To let the poets weave their immortal songs.
And you are to us like the cause and purpose of life,
And how little you know how much we live with you by.

Is there any one who has heard of a country known as *Bharat*?
But where Ganga did not flow.
Is there any band of people seized by a purpose?
But who had no place to go.
And finally it was found that it was by you, mother Ganga,
That our land was known as *Bharat*,
Made great by your immortal flow.

Ganga, you flow on binding me with the unknown past
When many like me had their little dip.

And then they would have thought of the time when they would have passed,
As I now think of the time when I would be a part of the past.
But Ganga, you would be here to flow on as you did in the age-old past,
And all those who had bathed in the past, who are bathing now, and those in the unborn time,
All would be strung by the common bond of your purity unsurpassed.

# XLIX

# My Most Beloved Motherland

My most beloved motherland,
Many a dream had I cherished, many a hope had I treasured;
Forces of reaction threaten these with extinction.

Where has that language disappeared that held us together?
Did we not speak many languages when we were not free?
Where has that voice disappeared that we spoke as one nation?
Did we not have many viewpoints when we were in bondage?

Was this land not inhabited by so many religions?
That we quarrel over religions that have found here a shelter.
There were innumerable castes and boundaries when we were not divided;
Why should boundaries be our barriers, and castes the cause of hate?

We did not fight for freedom to revert to slavery;
Why should doubts visit our minds when we should be united?

When we were in bondage, when we were not free,

We had one hope and one dream, our land must be free.
Our people must share fully the fruits of their labours.
Our views should find respect and our voice should be heard.

What is then this haste, why are we going yonder?
Let us wait for a while, let us pause and ponder.
There could be a voice of reason, we must examine our hearts.
We must preserve our unity against fissiparous ideas.
Our land could hold us one when suffering for a common cause;
Cannot we conserve our freedom in face of so many onslaughts?

# The Republic Day

Today, long before the break of dawn,
Long before the night took leave of sleep,
Long before the town had time to have stretched itself to a little rest,
I was awakened by the clatter of feet,
By the babble of men, women and children in full abandon;
By the entire transport of the town making a variegated march,
By the fast dash of cars and by the overtaking bravely driven taxies,
By the immense number of men on foot, singing and frolicking,
By a large number of beings carried in the air through scooters and *phut-phut*,
And those who were in no hurry
Being carried merrily in the crimson canopied decorated carts,
Led by determined and strong bullocks
With their bells jingling on their necks and feet.
The entire multitude being fully conscious of the importance of the day,
And finally becoming part of an endless stream and being pushed on their way.
Even the dogs keeping quiet, though entrusted to keep in safe custody the silence of the night.
On such a night I was awakened to see what was happening outside.
What I saw, opened my eyes.
I realized then, as I had never done before,
The love and enthusiasm of our people for our motherland.

Today, ten years past, the power that belonged to kings
Had been passed on to the women and men.
And all, each one of them, had become as big as any king,
And thus our first Republic was born.

To celebrate the day, in dedication of the day,
When each one of the men became symbol of great strength,
Possessing in his hands his rights denied to him for centuries;
When he became free to converse, to express and to discourse;
And when the collective will of men became the nation's law,
That all the men muster together, the millions of them,
Everywhere all over the land, to herald the dawn of our freedom,

The masses of men are converging,
Coming from long distances to the focal point—
To the place where the vast assembly sits,
To watch the procession of our armed men
March to martial tunes.
Serious, determined men to show the charge they hold of our country's defence,
And how they, each one of them, by displaying the types of tanks, guns,
Planes, and other symbols of our mighty strength,
Would save the motherland, keep flying the flag of our freedom,
And hold high the pride and prestige or our beloved motherland.

And thus wearing themselves a part of the pride of freedom,
These women and men celebrate the Republic Day.

## LI

# *Young ascetic, why do you exasperate me into defeat?*

Young ascetic, why do you exasperate me into defeat?
Why do you wear this stern look?
You were not cast in stone but in flesh and blood,
Then why do you bear this cold look?

You little know that you were born like a flower in the garden of my desires.
Like a flower you were to be first a bud, shy, quiet and secretive,
And then you were slowly to open the petals of your youth,
And it would have been for me to admire the different hues,
To smell your erotic aroma, to be struck by your inviting smiles,
And to have plucked you to lie in the velvety folds of my bosom,
And to have drunk deep from your sweet nectar,
And to have moved across the world, carrying the stamp of my fulfillment.

But, young ascetic, you seem determined to defy me.
In trying to overlook me you are ignoring nature.
Ascetic, do you know that you cannot defy nature?
For, nature is more powerful than your scornful looks.
Don't you know that you are yourself a product of nature?

And how much so ever you may show your strength of unconcern,
And delude yourself on your achievement of showing your unconcern,
That strength is also provided by nature.
For what are you wearing this mask of superficiality?
Whom are you going to impress by this artificiality?
Don't you know that nature that let you wear this mask of pretence
Has so far excused you as a child having lost his way?
It can also remove this false pretence,
Reduce you to the nakedness of reality,
Envelop you in its bosom,
Spread round you tentacles of its ties,
And put you to such use for which it created you.
Thus, be not misled to believe
That off-springs of nature could be stronger than the source of their strength,
And further have the audacity to defy its designs.

Look at me.
I am a woman.
I am a product of nature and a part of nature,
And I never lose my contact with the world of nature.
I remain ever attuned to nature
And get from it all my strength and response.
I was created by nature to be a cause of procreation
And nature creates everything for further creation.
All round I see the romance of creation.
I see all around birds, animals, flowers, fruits and trees.
I see these as examples of the world of creation.
For what purpose would have been rains and seeds,
And for what purpose would have been air and sun
Without the mother earth
On which stands the entire edifice of civilization.

The same is the place of woman in the world of creation,
And like earth, she bears the burden of creation,
And gives the world its present shape and pattern.

Young ascetic, do you know it was woman who first came in the world?
To join the world in one perpetual bond,
The bond by which has been achieved the present stage of development.
Ascetic, woman arrived in the world to give a start to the world
And to perpetuate the law of creation.
Now the world is on an accelerated pace
Because of the pivotal role woman was assigned to play.
Woman has ever remained the pivot round which the world rotates,
And though we live in a man's world, yet it is round a woman that it rotates.
Don't you know that beauty, colour and gaiety were born for a woman?
For, who else in nature decorates itself better than a woman,
And for whom does a man produce and create everything except for a woman.
The armaments of war and the triumphs of science and machines
Have often gone to obliterate man's own working.
A woman remains ever grateful to the man who does anything special for her,
And always her body's rapture expresses that for her.
Does not a woman, full of beauty and grace, ever enrich a man's life and purpose?
Does not a woman,
Donning colours copied from nature and created by man,

Wearing jewels excavated from earth and chiselled by man,
Get a unique power and strength?
And does not that woman
Rule over the hearts of men?
In return she gives herself up to the man who makes her his beloved and the lovely one.
It is the crowning of these activities that gives civilization its permanent existence;
That lets man find a secured employment,
And that saves him from being deployed on missions of destruction.

Ascetic, men have often carried the world to the brink of its destruction.
Men have been often sworn to enmity for the sake of divisions.
Men have often made many resolves for the sake of resolutions.
All these activities have carried men no further to any achievement.
Only woman has provided man with a permanent reason.
Only her inspiration has saved the world from its sure destruction.
Ascetic, the existence of the world finds its echo in the aspirations of a woman.
Her arrival in the world is a positive assurance of its continuity.
And in secret chambers of her bosom are concealed
Sproutings of the urge to re-create.
Her whole being is ever bound with the world of eternity,
And she ever comes and ever goes
To the call of that eternal message.
Behind you ascetic, and behind every man, stands the

eternal woman,
And for every man, ascetic, there is an eternal woman,
Ensuring and securing for herself her own perpetuity.

Ascetic, I have come to you for you to surrender yourself to my eternity,
And give up yourself to me for my continuity.
Ascetic, no man has ever had any individual existence,
And every man who prides himself for his independent existence,
Was once neither an individual nor ever independent,
For, he was then caged in the womb of an expectant woman.

Ascetic, you are sitting here as if having been over-burdened with the weight of living,
And you wanted an escape where you could make light your own living,
And could spend your time away from the thunder and clash of living.
Ascetic, the burden of living is carried by woman and not by man.
It should have been woman who should have renounced the world,
Forsaken it for its miseries and tragedies,
Given it up for its pains and privacies,
Hated it for its diseases and disasters,
Run away from it for its cruelties and tyrannies,
Condemned it for its vices and vengeances,
And revolted against it for its barbarity and violence.
But, ascetic, woman forbears everything,
She puts up with life's all adversities;
She faces difficult times and climes.
And she fights unknown and uncertain future
Because she is herself the embodiment of the cause of

living,
Because she knows that she alone cannot shape the state of her living,
Because she realizes her limited role in life's endless ways,
And thus she accepts everything as it comes in her way.
In her nature, she does not believe in evolving methods to escape,
And she knows that it is her burden to carry the world's weight;
And she carries it joyously and graciously, leading the world from age to age.

Ascetic, man has had his way throughout the ages.
He did what he ever wanted to do.
He enslaved other women and men and killed them by millions.
Pages of history are darkened by his deeds of ghastly butchery.
His spirit of revenge knows not the limit of its satisfaction.
While you ascetic, you sit here pretending to atone for the evils of countless centruries
By trying to escape from the ties of nature and its beauties,
And making light the burden of your living by this silly renunciation.
What have you done for the world to qualify for this stature?
It is woman who has given this world the surety of its existence.
It is she who repays the debts to bountiful nature,
And it is she who discharges the liabilities incurred by the wrath of man.
It is she who conceives in hope and rears her children,

And it is she who returns to bountiful nature what she ever receives from it.
She alone leads a complete and dedicated life
To the cause of making this world a lovely and beautiful thing.

But man hardly does anything,
He gives not to nature the best of his being.
He looks upon nature as a tantalizing mystery,
And without understanding the qualities of nature and its beings,
And without getting from it the benefits he can always receive,
He jumps headlong to unravel behind nature, its mystery.
Wanting to know why is behind nature any mystery;
And why is behind him even a mystery;
And why should there be any mystery in mystery;
And why should there at all be any mystery.

Young ascetic! Why do you do this penance?
Is it to delve deep into that mystery that you do this penance?
What is that cause of the universe that you wish to serve through this penance?
Or is it to increase your knowledge that you do this penance?
Will your spiritual strength increase through this penance?
Why do you deny yourself the strength gifted to you by nature,
And adopt artificial means to add to your strength?
To what purpose would you put this strength?
Were you not strong enough to face the world?
Were you not strong enough to give me your love?

What is the strength that you lacked that you are now trying to possess?
Were you not possessed of sufficient knowledge acquired at the feet of your *gurus*?
That you chose to discover any new light by inflicting this self-suffering.
You may become the wisest among men,
And may put a new meaning to the mysteries of the universe.
Of what value will be that wisdom and to what use will you put that wisdom.
In my eyes, young ascetic, your wisdom will be like artificial flowers,
Not able to replace the exquisite and throbbing beauty of nature.

Look at me, I get all my wisdom from nature
Which is profound, meaningful and greatly true.
Don't you see that deriving my strength and wisdom from nature I remain true to nature?
I love colour, beauty and grace of nature.
I live like nature and dress like nature.
I love like nature and give myself up to one
Who, like nature, welcomes and accepts one without reservation.
Thus, my wisdom is grounded in nature, fed by nature and supported by nature.
Now, let me look at your wisdom.
You add to your wisdom by deductions to your many suppositions.
Your knowledge has a meaning so long as it stands on artificial foundations.
Your knowledge is profound so long as its theories and precepts remain unchallenged,
But once new concepts are born, old views crumble like

heaps of corn.
Roots of your knowledge go not deep in the ground,
But are scattered on the surface all round.
My knowledge is as old as nature, as permanent as the universe;
As deep-rooted as nature and as much full of purpose,
And therefore, young ascetic, I can laugh at your shallowness,
Smile at your seriousness, and feel amused at your assumed concern.
For me, your knowledge is like airy bubbles;
Your penance like the obstinacy of a spoilt child,
And your determination like that of a buffoon in a comic opera.

Ascetic! Nature will have its revenge on you.
You are defying its laws,
Thinking you are more powerful than what sustains you.
You are drawing from it more than what you are giving back to it.
You are drawing from it water, air and sun.
You are drawing from it everything else that helps you in your sustenance.
Nature brought you here for its own fulfillment
That you will serve its cause as its instrument,
And participate in its glory, joy and abandon,
And become in its vast and grand order a piece of decoration.
Nature would have then claimed, "Here is my specimen."
In its colorful panorama of endless patterns
Nature would have placed you before the world as its present.
But here you are living in complete isolation,
Not even giving back to nature enough to keep up its balance.

In burning your flesh and blood you are sapping the tenderness of your freshness.
What is destroyed cannot be re-created.
What is lost cannot be recovered.
Ascetic, you are wasting the time of your destiny.
There is the voice of future beckoning you,
Calling you to itself and wanting you to march ahead.
It has with it a box containing record of everyone's waste,
And at proper time the future will open the box,
Show you how you had failed to perform your tasks,
And wasted your precious future which by then would have turned into past.
You would then see how every second you had, had been consumed in sheer aimlessness;
How you had been cruel with present and ignored its preciousness.
Therefore, future is warning you not to let present slip into past,
Yet you sit unmoved, though surrounded by piles of wasted past.

What is that fear that keeps you back from blossoming as a flower?
Are you afraid that urge of nature will unmask your artificial seriousness?
And that you may face yourself the naked urge to love and be loved;
And that may show you as a helpless creature before powerful nature;
And failed in your mission to prove your mantle as a superman.
And young ascetic, reduced as a man, you may be shorn of your celibacy,
And then you may become as much a part of nature as I

am.
Ascetic, celibacy does not exist in nature, being foreign to its qualities.
How can you exist in nature if you do not do your duty?
Ascetic, I know not why need you try to be a superman,
When you first did not try to be an ordinary man.
Ascetic, though man was born to be a man and woman, woman,
Yet man was not born to fulfill a mission different from a woman,
Nor was his role to be superior to that of a woman.
What really happened was that woman came first,
Being the cause behind nature;
And man followed her as a partner to let woman fulfill her functions,
While you, ascetic, you sit before me like a frame cast into stone,
Serving just no function.

Young ascetic, the present civilization is not a result of any one's penance,
Nor of any one's wisdom.
What exists is what was saved by a woman;
What has disappeared is what was destroyed by a man.

Ascetic, your approach is negative in conception.
You are the same whether you take to sword and fight a war
Or take to celibacy and do some penance.
For me you are a victim of your cruel destructive self,
When you imagine you can attain any higher wisdom
By cutting yourself from nature and love and tenderness of a woman;
When you indulge in narrow-mindedness;
When you fight over airy and intellectual arguments;

When you think another one should not have taken your possessions;
When you see another person has in hand an inch more of your land;
When you find another one speaking with a different argument;
When you come across another one in different colour or form,
And when sometimes for no reason you hate and destroy another one.
To me a man appears to be possessed by an evil spirit
Whenever he turns his back on nature, and seeks other routes of fulfillment;
Whenever he takes to a cult or an ism and pursues it blindly;
Whenever he fixes his faith in ritualism and thinks that that will give him salvation;
Whenever he believes not that birth is for living and not for suicide;
Whenever he learns not from other beings like animals, flowers and trees;
Whenever he sees not that other creatures seek their fulfillment by living in this world.
Ascetic, contemplate for a while that if flowers and trees, birds and animals
Had decided to delve deep into nature's mysteries and done some penance,
And if these sproutings of nature had decided to waste their form and shed their qualities,
What would have the world done, and how would have the humans lived?
Ascetic, the world exists because all forms of nature do their entrusted tasks,
But you sit here lost, nursing some unknown grievance,
And causing yourself so much physical and emotional

imbalance,
And thinking that this desolate path will lead you to the end of some bliss.
Ascetic, your mind, musing in the desert of non-existence,
Showing disregard and disrespect to nature's other forms,
Can only get a blank and vacant response from its penance.
In the end of your penance you would gain nothing,
For, your penance is pursuing the cause of nothingness.
Ascetic, you understand not that if you close your mind to fresh air;
If you take to negative thinking;
If you deny your mind the echo that it can get from nature;
If you learn not from other manifestations of creative force
That they by living joyously and freely are fulfilling its object,
How can you by ignoring its call be a part of the world?
Nature will deny you its benevolence if you deny it your participation.
In its curse you will lose your perception and be another part of dust for it.

Ascetic, your penance is perverse in conception.
You only try and withdraw your mind and heart, eyes and ears, flesh and body from activity,
And you think your system trained to this withdrawal,
Sitting like an insect in a small cocoon,
Is a protection from the evil of living,
And by this you would reach a high level of spiritual strength.
Ascetic, you are mistaken if you imagine that
Soul can get its fulfillment when it is denied its

nourishment.
Soul is in communion with the spirit of creation that prevails in the universe.
How can you, by ignoring your own creative urges, seek any fulfillment?
How can you, by destroying the qualities of that spirit, give it any pleasure?
That spirit expects its objects to live with one another in harmony,
To experience bliss and joy in living and to find in one's spirit its response.
The spirit of creation operates unimpeded in everything living that exists,
And seeks an echo from other beings in which it operates.
In you it sought an expression but the spirit had a dazzle;
Now frightened by that dazzle you stand in its way.
To deny the spirit of creation an outlet of its release,
You seek refuge under a deception that may pass till it lasts.
If a tree is not allowed to grow out as its branches might be big,
The spirit of creation will damage the surroundings to let out the tree to grow.
The spirit in you needed a large exit of the size of your creative urge,
But you decided to narrow your conception by preventing its escape.
Dear ascetic, the love that rose in your heart had threatened to thunder,
You should have let the clouds gather their force and break out in their rain.
It would have brought spring to your life
And you would have become a part of its delight.
In its wildness and abandon

You would have experienced an endless joy.
In its beauty and riot of colour
You would have felt an ecstasy.
The floods brought by rain would have been the overflowing heart in its love,
And you would have found in the spirit of creation the counterpart of your love.
Instead of chosing the way of the world you chose to confine yourself,
Confine yourself to the imprisonment of your narrow-mindedness.

If you, ascetic, withdraw your body and mind from the world and stay in suspense,
What will you achieve by that denial and whose cause will you fulfil?
Soul operates only through that body which it occupies,
How can you destroy that body and think that soul will be pleased?
Ascetic, in the flights of pure fancies nothing has been ever achieved.
Return to this earth, mother earth, that gave you birth.
See what is around you and seek from it a meaning;
Be a part of the universe and get from it your strength.
If you pursue your lonely path, you will reach nowhere.
At present you are seized by a hypnotism sustained by self-deception.
That will disappear as soon as your age and mood would change.
You would, to keep your mind closed from having any other experience,
Evolve some other methods that could continue this self-imposed deception.
Out of all these rigours of self-infliction you might evolve a new approach;

Out of the trials and tribulations you pass through, you might bring out a new point;
But all these pursuits of pure intellect are meaningless phenomena.
Your mind can only think conditioned by a relativity;
No one can ever think of anything in an absolute vacuum.
So your mind will return to objects that are around you,
And you would find objects necessary so long as you want to live and think.
One day the deception now serving you will turn into your enemy,
When nature will surround you with its bounty and have on you its revenge.

Ascetic, you are listening not to my knowledge acquired from nature.
You are trying to live in a desert where nothing ever exists.
What you see is a mirage created by your own deception,
And it will slip away farther, farther to it you go.
I live attached to nature and procreate this world.
So I know where there is an oasis and where there is a desert.
Come and quench your thirst from this well existing in this world.
Young ascetic, it is for nothing that I stopped in your way.
I was going along my path absorbed in my thoughts
That I saw you cross-legged in a wistful mood,
Trying to penetrate into some deep mystery.
You are young in age, and a thought flashed in my mind.
"So handsome, so strong, he looks near the ideal of a maiden's dreams.
"One who could satisfy a forlorn woman's longings."
But here you sat in a quaint way absorbed in some

ecstasy.
Your looks, your youth challenged my overflowing youth.
What was that that had forced you to adopt this lonely path?
Why had you not taken to the world and become a part of its stream?
Then I wondered why it was that you stayed away from the stream?
You are young, too young, to have been betrayed by any woman,
And no woman would have, without being mad,
Betrayed a man who could be so much near her heart.
And thus I thought that because of some foolish ideas
You had been made to pursue this path.
It was not for showing you small,
Nor it was for displaying the powers of a woman
That I stood before you,
Gaping in amazement about what you are.
A storm made my heart leap at your youth.
I found your countenance chiding me that only a man could be his own,
That he alone could forsake everything and ignore the world's attractions,
And then parade himself as a superman with great achievements
Of having succeeded in the impossibility of living without a woman.
Ascetic, if a man has to give up the world for giving up a woman,
I wonder what is more important, the world or a woman.
In any case if a woman is a handicap to your existence,
You should better take the woman than give up your existence.
It is for this I have sat before you,

Trying to deflect you from your deserted path,
And to persuade you to walk with me in the garden of my desires.

I know not what has been driven into your head
That nothing leaves on you any effect.
I am not here to entrap you with momentary magic of my beauty
Nor am I here to entrance you with my soft and silken caresses.
I could have tried this and you would have been mine.
But any one with greater beauty and strength
Would have bound you with her superior designs.
I want to awake in your heart bonds of the world of growth;
I want to revive memories of the time when you came alone,
And when you were a babe
And only your mother could wipe the tears from your face;
When you cried to satisfy your hunger and thirst,
And only what your mother gave you let you feel at rest.
You grew before her watchful eyes as her darling son,
And hope of her future days.
And then your elder sister also grew with you,
And in her you found another example of woman's qualities.
You also saw how she one day went away as a bride from your house
To bedeck someone else's dreams.
On growing up, you became an ascetic, forsaking your dear mother,
And forgetful of the love and tender bonds of your loved sister,
Breaking all your ties with the women who nursed you

and fondled you.
These woman had seen you grow from boyhood to youth
With keen, observant eyes.
They had felt the thrill how their own darling every year became
Bigger and bigger in size.
They became confident everyday that one's brother and the other's son
Would bring to the family unity, strength and pride.
As he advanced in age, they thought, he was growing to be a man.
He would be a helpful, wise, kind and devoted man.
But having ripened into manhood he ceased to be a man,
And ran away to escape from the strength and power of man.

Why do you want to run away from reality to a world of shadows?
Why do you wish to seek your shelter under an umbrella of shadows?
What you see as protection, is actually a deception.
The theories you imagine would give you peace, are merely a conception.
They cut away all your connections with the world of reality,
And you are wrong to feel you have reached a high level of ecstasy.
Ascetic, you are wrong if you think that
In being surrounded by a vacuum of loneliness
You are in communion,
By believing in the hollow philosophy of doing nothing
You have reached the goal of life,
And in sitting here like a statue
You are serving any cause of life.
Ascetic, being products of creative energy we are born to

re-create,
And there can be no creative activity till we play our role in life.
We should follow the path inspired by the spirit of creation,
And that path requires every one to join in the game of life.
If no one ever did anything how would have the world at all existed,
Neither you would have been born nor I would have come to life.
You were born as an expression of the spirit of creation,
Containing within yourself the energy to sprout and regenerate.
Why do you sit here as a statue sulking with frustration,
Without having tasted the fruit of life in its passion and its grace?
Having denied yourself an outlet of your creative expression,
You see everything as an illusion out to disturb your poised state.
You have withdrawn from the world of nature full of boundless creation,
And sought refuge in a blankness where all would vanish to waste.
As an instrument of creation you have been lost to nature,
And nature would adapt itself to the situation that its efforts went in vain.
You may ignore the will of creation but nature will not forsake you,
It will let you live and serve you even in your cast off state.
It will let you breathe and eat and let you sleep,
And sustain you to the best of its capacity even in your

handicapped state.

I am a woman, I know what sustains a woman's life.
I cannot deny myself the role I have to play.
I know that drawing sustenance from nature,
Like any other animal, bird, flower, or living thing,
I am a part of the manifestation of nature,
And I have to fulfil my role assigned to me by nature.
I have to be a part of nature and blossom like a flower,
To be loved, to be admired, and to beautify the world;
And like any living thing of nature to play my role and return to nature,
And then come again to be a part of the world.
Thus I move about fulfilling my role prescribed by nature,
And as an expression of creative energy at its best in the world.

I propound no theories of life.
I need no philosophies to explain the mysteries of life.
I take my inspiration from nature and for me it is a simple life.
There is no mystery in nature that is not to every one known.
It is easy to observe, easy to understand, and easy to comprehend.
I remain ever bound to nature and I ignore everything else of no consequence.
I share its beauties, share its delights and share its songs,
Become fully a part of it, live in it, and die singing its songs.

But you, ascetic, sit at a high pedestal,
Having chosen a different path,
Unconcerned of nature, of your role and of your past,

Obsessed by an idea that nature may destroy what is good,
And promote what is evil in the world.
And therefore, you are doing this penance to preserve the good in the world,
And prevent nature from having its way.
But what is that that nature seeks, and what is that that you seek:
Nature having nursed you in its cradle wants you to grow;
But you are misled to seek its Maker, Master and Poet.
Forsaking what nature is, ignoring the will of the Maker, Master and Poet.
You want to seek the world by renouncing it,
And to seek bliss in the world by running away from it.
The world is too large for any one to run away from it.
By cutting short your stay you can run away from it.
But living in the world you are a part of it.
There is no other world you can reach by running away from it.
Even by running away from it you continue to breathe,
You continue to eat and sleep.
And what is this artificial manner of running away from it,
When you live in it?
If you live in it, you are a part of it.
If you are a part of it,
How are you then away from it?

Wherever you may go, whatever you may do,
Nature will be there to greet you.
In the snow-laden mountains of Himalayas
Or in the large deserts of Rajasthan,
In the dark forests of Assam
Or in the lovely beauty of our country's many places;

Wherever you go you will find nature.
Everywhere nature will give you air, light, water and food.
The insects, birds and animals will greet you in their mirth and glee,
The children will be overflowing with peals of laughter,
And women will be full of grace, charm and beauty.

Ascetic, nature and its beings will not shed their qualities
Only because you want your eyes not to see what exists,
Your nose not to smell what pervades,
Your body not to touch what it feels,
And your ears not to hear what is audible.
Ascetic, having been gifted with the qualities of living,
You want to acquire the role of a statue;
Reducing yourself to the status of being nothing
You want to be something.
Ascetic, your present efforts will lead you nowhere.
Your meaningless pursuits cannot bear any fruit.
You cannot acquire godliness by sheer renunciation.
You cannot add to your spiritual strength in a vacuum.
Your actions are like trying to grow vegetation in a desert.
You are trying to climb high without any stairs.
Pray, ascetic, take counsel from what you are.
Do not, swept by silly and make-believe subtleties,
Tread a path that only acts like a mirage.
The strange subtlety that occupies your heart was a creation of your conflicting mind.
And you, without tasting the fruit of life, have been led to tread a wrong path.

Ascetic, looking at your senseless pursuits
I am led to believe a woman is superior to a man.
The men who hold women in sway of their strength;

Who subjugate them, who maltreat them;
Who deny them their honoured place, and who show their brutal force
Against gentle and tender beings,
Cannot match their qualities to these of a woman
Who needs no such force to keep man bound in her enchanting spell.
But what does a man gain by such maltreatment and subjugation?
At best he shows his prowess of physical strength.
But what has man ever achieved by display of his strength?
Other men with superior strength
Have ever scored over men with lesser power of resistance.
But woman has never had any need to develop her muscular strength.
She never has to call the aid of violence,
Whether for being able to deal with other women
Or for keeping any number of men under her influence.
She has ever dealt with them through her innate strength.
She has given men the cause of their existence
And has held men under her absolute dominion.
She has ever got other women's concurrence for her common cause,
The cause of being a woman.
Have you ever heard a woman ever killing a woman?
But score-board of man shows
Men killing other men, women and children by millions.
And thus, am I wrong, if I say that woman is a much superior person?
And yet what is a man?
How far has he stood out as a man?
How much can he show himself as a man?
How few have been men

Who could practise a woman's natural qualities?
How few men have displayed disinterested love and compassion?
Only a few rare souls among men could be spiritually awakened;
And they after much penance and penetration,
Could discover only this truth—
That what saves the world is love and compassion—
Qualities that come naturally to a woman.
Ascetic, there is no higher wisdom that you can acquire through this penance
Than the wisdom that is the inherent strength of a woman.
Ascetic, be not disturbed by my frank and plain talk.
I sometimes feel shocked that you are limiting your role in nature's tasks.
Nature has put up with man's vanity and tyranny only to perpetuate itself.
But if man goes on pursuing his present path;
And if he attunes not himself to nature's purpose;
If he continues to demand penalty and price for his job,
Nature may take its revenge and through him obliterate the entire world.
Ascetic, that would be a sad end to your penance.
For, in a lifeless world there would be no cause for any penance.
Ascetic, there is no cause and no world that you can serve through this penance.
For, the world full of living has to be lived
And, the world of lifelessness is useless for living.
What world would you reach by doing this penance?
You must play your part in nature
And keep yourself absorbed in its tasks.
As long as you are a part of this world,
You should remain true to its cause,

For, you are subordinate to nature, being one of its parts.

Ascetic, if you only cared to see the realities that subsist in this world;
Ascetic, only if you were alive to its actualities
You would find that wherever a man may go;
Whatever he may strive to do;
It is he who comes to a woman by himself.
It is he who returns to her,
Whether he may have earned laurels for rare courage and fortitude in a battle field;
Whether he may have amassed all the wealth he could ever dream of;
Whether he may have reached the summit of his glory, greatness, and strength;
Whether he may have scored the triumph of his ambitions
Or he may have made the final surrender to his failures;
He comes back to a woman.
He returns to her after being slighted in an argument;
After having been injured in a fight;
After having been defeated in a war,
And after having lost all he possessed.
And whenever he seeks a mental balance,
Shattered by divided thinking,
He gets his composure from the commonsense of a woman;
And thus everywhere, every man comes back to a woman.
But you, ascetic, you claim to be a different man
By remaining away from a woman.
In this world, with women constituting half its population
There is no escape from a woman.
Ascetic, granted you may succeed in your penance.

Even granted, you may break the chains of repeated births
And be blessed with *moksha*,
How would the other men succeed in their mission?
How would they achieve their *moksha*
If women were not to conceive and deliver all the men?
Ascetic, by your celibacy you may succeed in not leaving any inheritance,
But that deliverance will be merely of a physical form.
How are you assured of your spiritual deliverance by burning your physical form?
Ascetic, if renunciation could be a passport to salvation,
And denial of comforts to body and mind any special achievement,
Those sick and those suffering from poverty and misery would be nearer the state of *moksha*.
Ascetic, you cannot separate your physical form from the state of your mind.
You cannot kill one to ensure the bliss of the other.
Ascetic, the path followed by you contradicts the aim to be achieved by you.
The bliss you aim at is denied by the methods adopted by you.
Ascetic, be a man and draw from the world the substance of its existence.
Ascetic , women in the world are not meant to be shunned as impure ones.
For, there is nothing pure and impure about a woman.
Every woman is ever pure like nature which remains ever pure.
No woman can ever be tarnished by accusation of the sly.
For, is not purity itself born from the pains of her deliverance?
Every one she gives birth to is born pure,
And one giving birth is ever doubly pure.

Woman is the purest product of God.
For, she reflects truly the state of His designs,
And in her is found the embodiment of His mercy and compassion,
And she alone ensures the glory of His vast kingdom.
It is woman alone who takes the tenderest care of her children,
And rears forth her offspring to let them be fully grown as men and women.
Having nursed them and having given them her care, love and her entire whole,
She lets nature accept her offspring as her gift to the world.
To let her children join the vast multitude and become a part of nature's streams,
Giving themselves upto nature, and ever dreaming in its dreams.

Ascetic, woman has never sought to secure for herself any privilege or position.
She arrives to be a part of nature and is welcomed by nature.
She departs, saying her farewell to nature
When she ceases to be of use to nature.
Deriving from nature her qualities,
Getting from it her sustenance,
Being inspired by it for her aim and goal,
She is ever enriching it by her powerful role.

Ascetic, the world of man is foreign to a woman.
She needs no trappings of civilization.
She is not running the exterior of our civilization.
She is not normally found in a government.
And may I ask you, why do men need a government?
Why do they need the rules of a game?

Why do they need these chains of social customs?
All because men cannot live as one.
All because they can easily quarrel over an argument.
They can easily divide other men over colour, race and form.
They can easily hate for the sake of hating another one.
To keep them away from breaking one another's heads,
They themselves set a limit to one another's activities,
And now by complicating the set of rules, they call it a government.
For having no other activity they make new social customs.
But a woman has no use of a government.
A woman has no use of social customs.
She has no need of all the rituals that were made by men.

A woman would have run the world without a government.
She would have made living a simple honest thing.
She would have lived like other beings without any daily strifes.
She would not have waged wars with bloody and deadly weapons.
She would not have killed other men by millions.
She would not have subjected men to untold tyranny.
She would not have made living a hard and hated thing.
But men, free from the throes of bearing children,
Free from woman's caring and anxious nature,
Free from woman's love for silent and quiet living,
Full of burning curiosity,
Full of fire for revenge,
Full of uninhibited urge for adventure,
Provoked and disturbed by the deep mystery of nature,
Set out before themselves the task of unraveling the world,

And what they could not unravel, of taming that part of the world,
Of taming rivers, sea, air, sun and animals,
And to taming the remainder of everything in the universe.
When men looked at a simple thing as a woman,
They found her deeply disturbing and full of agonizing mystery.
They discovered, she possessed great power and mystery.
First they tried to unravel that mystery,
But having failed to solve that mystery,
And being concerned at her subtle and superior strength,
And being jealous of her unmatched importance
They thought of taming the woman
And deprive her of her womanliness.
In the process they looked at themselves
And found that they could not do without a woman,
And felt shocked and mad at this prospect
That a man should ever feel weak and meek before a woman;
Thus they decided that they should first tame themselves.

Ascetic, you are only an example of a man's attempt to tame himself.
Yes, to deny himself the urge to love and to be loved,
To deprive himself of the senses to feel, see, hear and smell.
Instead of meeting the challenge of your manliness,
Ascetic, you are depriving yourself of the Man—
And to be left like a statue in flesh and blood.

Young ascetic, you have proved weak as a man.
You are not a man.
I am woman, the strength behind man,
Like one whose flesh you carry.

I am the cause of birth, the purpose behind the universe.
You were born only as an instrument to perpetuate my strength,
You were born only as a link in the universe.
I am the *Shakti*, I am the power.
Ascetic, rise, you will serve no purpose by this penance.
Isolation will only bring decay
And break from this world will bring death.

You were born in this world, be a part of it.

# Glossary

| | |
|---|---|
| Ahimsa | Sanskrit word meanig non-violence |
| Bakra | Mutiple system of hydel power and irrigation canals |
| Bhangra | A local dance in Punjab |
| Bharat(a) | Another name of India |
| Dharma | Sanskrit word meaning Moral Code of Conduct |
| Gurus | Sanskrit word meaning teachers |
| Holi | Festival of Colour in India |
| Holi Hai | Translates as "It is Holi" |
| Karma | Sanskrit word meaning righteous action |
| Karmayoga | Sanskrit word meaning righteous action aligned with spiritual purpose |
| Kikli | A local game in Punjab |
| Moksha | Sanskrit word meaning immortality |
| Paramatma | Sanskrit word meaning God |
| Phut-Phut | A local form of transport |
| Shakti | Sanskrit word meaning inner power and strength |

www.ingramcontent.com/pod-product-compliance
Lightning Source LLC
Chambersburg PA
CBHW020929090426
42736CB00010B/1082